THE **COMPLETE IDIOT'S GUIDE®** TO

Sailing

by Diane Selkirk

ALPHA

A member of Penguin Group (USA) Inc.

For Maia and Evan—the perfect crew in sailing and life.

ALPHA BOOKS

Published by Penguin Group (USA) Inc.

Penguin Group (USA) Inc., 375 Hudson Street, New York, New York 10014, USA • Penguin Group (Canada), 90 Eglinton Avenue East, Suite 700, Toronto, Ontario M4P 2Y3, Canada (a division of Pearson Penguin Canada Inc.) • Penguin Books Ltd., 80 Strand, London WC2R 0RL, England • Penguin Ireland, 25 St. Stephen's Green, Dublin 2, Ireland (a division of Penguin Books Ltd.) • Penguin Group (Australia), 250 Camberwell Road, Camberwell, Victoria 3124, Australia (a division of Pearson Australia Group Pty. Ltd.) • Penguin Books India Pvt. Ltd., 11 Community Centre, Panchsheel Park, New Delhi—110 017, India • Penguin Group (NZ), 67 Apollo Drive, Rosedale, North Shore, Auckland 1311, New Zealand (a division of Pearson New Zealand Ltd.) • Penguin Books (South Africa) (Pty.) Ltd., 24 Sturdee Avenue, Rosebank, Johannesburg 2196, South Africa • Penguin Books Ltd., Registered Offices: 80 Strand, London WC2R 0RL, England

Copyright © 2013 by Alpha Books

International Standard Book Number: 978-1-61564-2-403
Library of Congress Catalog Card Number: 2012949170

15 14 13   8 7 6 5 4 3 2 1

Interpretation of the printing code: The rightmost number of the first series of numbers is the year of the book's printing; the rightmost number of the second series of numbers is the number of the book's printing. For example, a printing code of 13-1 shows that the first printing occurred in 2013.

Printed in the United States of America

Note: This publication contains the opinions and ideas of its author. It is intended to provide helpful and informative material on the subject matter covered. It is sold with the understanding that the author and publisher are not engaged in rendering professional services in the book. If the reader requires personal assistance or advice, a competent professional should be consulted.

The author and publisher specifically disclaim any responsibility for any liability, loss, or risk, personal or otherwise, which is incurred as a consequence, directly or indirectly, of the use and application of any of the contents of this book.

Most Alpha books are available at special quantity discounts for bulk purchases for sales promotions, premiums, fund-raising, or educational use. Special books, or book excerpts, can also be created to fit specific needs. For details, write: Special Markets, Alpha Books, 375 Hudson Street, New York, NY 10014.

Publisher: *Mike Sanders*

Executive Managing Editor: *Billy Fields*

Executive Acquisitions Editor: *Lori Cates Hand*

Development Editor: *Michael Thomas*

Senior Production Editor: *Janette Lynn*

Copy Editor/Proofreader: *Cate Schwenk*

Cover Designer: *Kurt Owens*

Book Designers: *William Thomas, Rebecca Batchelor*

Indexer: *Tonya Heard*

Layout: *Ayanna Lacey*

Illustrations: *Peter Bull © Dorling Kindersley*

Contents

Appendixes

Introduction

You've never sailed, but it seems exciting, and you'd like to try it out. Or maybe you've been out a few times, but you never understood why you were told to pull in a rope one minute and to let it go the next. Or maybe you boat with someone fairly regularly, but you're intimidated by what's going on, frightened by the idea of taking the wheel, or even feeling a bit queasy at the thought of raising a sail.

In any case, you want to learn more about sailing: how to prepare the boat to leave the dock; when to raise and trim the sails; what safety gear you really need aboard; where to find accurate weather reports and how to understand them.

This is the book for you.

But I have to say this right off the bat—no book can *teach* you how to sail. To learn to sail, you really need to be taught by an instructor aboard a boat. Sailing is a sport with many nuances, and for it to make sense, and for it to be safe, you need to actively learn the skills in this book from someone qualified to teach them (and I will tell you how to find the right instructor).

Consider this book a reference or a textbook. Perhaps it'll be the manual you turn to when you're trying to figure out how the heck you're supposed to adjust your sails when the wind is coming over the front end of your boat, or you'll pick it up when you want to double-check how to read a tide table or tie that certain knot.

And that's how it's designed to be read.

It's meant to be there when you need it. It's meant to answer your questions and explain why you need to pull in that rope and then let it go again. It's meant to be picked up, thumbed through, thought about, and then put down as you get back to actively sailing. Or dreaming about sailing.

It's meant to start you on what I hope will become a very long and enjoyable voyage.

How This Book Is Organized

The book is divided into three parts. Each part is self-contained so you can focus on the topics you need when you need them (though sailing really is the sum of its parts, and eventually you'll want to read through the entire book).

Part 1, Getting Started in Sailing, sets you off with some of the basic information you should know, and understand, before you step aboard a boat. You'll learn the terminology of boats and be introduced to the language of sailing. You'll also discover how the forces of nature (i.e., the wind and waves) work on your boat. I focus on weather, and how and why you should get an accurate forecast. And then I spend some time looking at tides and currents and how they can affect your sailing plans.

Part 2, Basic Boat Handling, puts you aboard the boat. You'll learn the basics of sailing—how to rig and hoist sails, and then how to set sail and steer through all the points of sail. I also cover all the skills you need in order to get out sailing—how to prepare a boat for departure and how to motor away from a dock. I also look at essential safety equipment and cover a few more advanced skills: anchoring, reducing sail, managing in bad weather, and getting a tow.

Part 3, Getting Where You're Going, progresses on to navigation and beyond. I look at traditional paper charts and how to use them. And then I cover the pros and cons of electronic navigation, including all the different types of electronics that are commonly found on sailboats. I also go through the rules of the road, covering who has right of way and what all those markers on the water actually mean. And I tackle knots and maintenance, and then explore the process of finding and buying a boat of your own.

Extras

To make the learning experience as clear as possible, I've highlighted lots of tips, facts, definitions, and safety pointers throughout the book. Look for the following sidebars to guide you along:

SAILOR'S WARNING

Like the old proverb says, there are certain signs (red in the morning) sailors need to be aware of and take warning from. These sidebars highlight safety information that you shouldn't miss.

BETTER BOATING

Not every skill is found in a textbook. Some tips, like the ones highlighted in these sidebars, are passed from one sailor to the next.

NAUTICAL KNOWLEDGE

Sailing is filled with useful bits of information, and I slip in some of these info bites throughout the book. Some are helpful, some are simply interesting.

DEFINITION

Throughout the book you find lists of words and their definitions—but occasionally I highlight a word or concept that either doesn't fit in a list or that's really important to understand.

Acknowledgments

First, I want to thank my husband Evan and daughter Maia, who embraced the project and promised we'd find a way to fit it into our already busy life. It's probably my turn to do dishes now.

I also want to thank the teachers who first taught me to sail. When I was a young girl, living in a very small town, I was given the tiller to a sailboat and an entire world opened up to me. Seriously, as soon as I figured out how the tiller worked it became a profound and life-changing moment.

So here's the thing with the rest of my thank you's—I am fortunate to be part of not one, but two exceptionally giving and generous communities: the writing community and the sailing community. And I have lists of people I'm grateful to that are too long to include.

But a special thank you to Peter Robson and Dale Miller, my editors at *Pacific Yachting*, who have let me explore my favorite topic and come through with assignments when I've needed them most; and to Carolyne and Peter Smith, Sarah Rose, Lola Brown, and Mark and Val Riegel for so many things; and to the crews of *S/V Totem, Whatcha Gonna Do, Britannia, Piko, Don Quixote, Connect Four, Hotspur, Mangoe, Renova, Savannah,* and *Running Shoe* for the information, inspiration, and miles shared. And to my mum—thanks for letting me sail away.

Special Thanks to the Technical Reviewers

The Complete Idiot's Guide to Sailing was reviewed by two experts who double-checked the accuracy of what you'll learn here, to help us ensure that this book gives you everything you need to know about sailing. Special thanks are extended to Behan and Jamie Gifford.

Jamie Gifford is a lifelong sailor who spent his formative years designing sails for Grand Prix racers, America's Cup boats, and megayachts. He later shifted from racing to cruising: since 2008, he and his wife Behan have been cruising in their sloop, *Totem*.

Behan Gifford graduated from tooling around lakes in a Sunfish to racing dinghies as a collegiate sailor. She subsequently traded racing for cruising, and can currently be found sailing her home around the world with Jamie and their children.

Trademarks

All terms mentioned in this book that are known to be or are suspected of being trademarks or service marks have been appropriately capitalized. Alpha Books and Penguin Group (USA) Inc. cannot attest to the accuracy of this information. Use of a term in this book should not be regarded as affecting the validity of any trademark or service mark.

Getting Started in Sailing

There is nothing—absolutely nothing—half so much worth doing as simply messing about in boats.

—Kenneth Grahame, *The Wind in the Willows*

Going sailing the first time is like visiting a foreign country. The language is different; even words you've heard before don't mean what you think they mean. And the things that should be familiar—the tide, the wind, the weather—are viewed from an entirely new perspective.

Part 1 is here to guide you through the initial strangeness of sailing. You learn the lingo and discover the names for all the parts of the boat as well as the names for the people who sail her (though it may take practice to keep all the definitions of the word "tack" straight).

You also discover how the forces of nature affect a sailboat; how tides create currents that can help or hinder your journey; and how the wind propels a boat to sail. And you learn practical skills such as how to estimate wind speed, read tide tables, and understand marine weather reports.

Before You Set Sail

In This Chapter

- Learning the lingo
- Knowing the parts of a sailboat
- Choosing your first sailing experience
- Chartering, racing, cruising—which is for you?
- Monohulls, multihulls, dinghies, day-sailers, and more

"Haul in the main, trim the jib, and prepare to tack!"

Huh?

Sailing is a sport that combines physics, fluid dynamics, aerodynamics, and, if you're a novice, a bunch of strange-sounding words that seem to equate to a whole lot of work—especially if your goal was to get out on the water on a sunny afternoon and enjoy the view.

Learning to sail is like learning a foreign language; first you have to learn the vocabulary, then you need to learn to speak in full sentences. Or, in the case of sailing, first you need to learn a bunch of new words, then you try to keep them straight while spray is flying over the *beam* (the widest part of the boat) and you're trying to remember what *grind* in the *starboard genoa sheet* (we'll get to this) actually means.

Speaking the Language

Fortunately, you've probably already heard many key sailing terms in everyday speech: *bow, lines, port, grind* (front of the boat, ropes used to control things, left side of the boat, using a winch to tighten a line)—you just thought they meant completely different things (half of a dog's bark, a punishment in school, a nice drink, getting beans ready for coffee).

Sailors have their own special archaic language for naming the parts and equipment found on a boat and for telling each other what to do with it. Learning the lingo early on means you'll never embarrass yourself by saying, "*I used the whatchamacallit to tighten up the thingamajig just like the whosamacallit said.*"

But before I offer up a few terms worth learning early on, let me explain in advance about the word *tack*. For whatever reason, in sailing, tack has several meanings, including turning the boat through the wind, a part of the sail (bottom forward corner), and the side of the boat the wind is coming from—as in *port tack*. And it can also mean what you think it means—you can tack a notice up on the marina's bulletin board.

Parts of the Hull

Starting with the hull (think body on a car), you can work on the obvious terms first: tiller = steering wheel; stern = back of the car; cockpit = front seats.

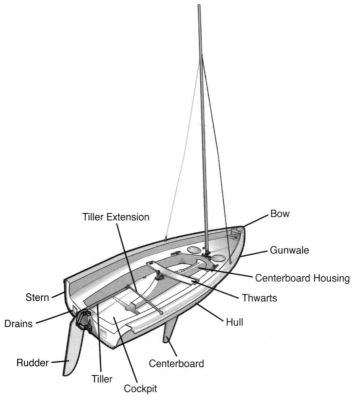

Parts of the hull: Dinghy.

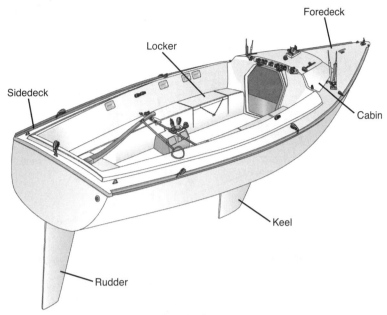

Parts of the hull: Keelboat.

The nice thing about sailboats is once you have the lingo down, it won't matter if you're on a dinghy or a luxury yacht—the basic vernacular is the same. You'll have a *hull* (the main structure of a boat), which may or may not have an interior cabin. Affixed to the hull will be a *rudder* (a moveable foil that steers the boat) as well as a *keel*, a retractable *centerboard*, or a *daggerboard* (foils located under the hull that provide lift, ballast and/or stability). And you'll have a *mast* with some arrangement of sails. On a luxury yacht you may also have a hot tub, big-screen TV, and an icemaker—but you know those terms.

Standing and Running Rigging

Looking up from the hull, the main structure on sailboats is the mast—it's supported by a variety of *spreaders* (horizontal struts coming off the mast) and *shrouds and stays* (wires holding up the mast).

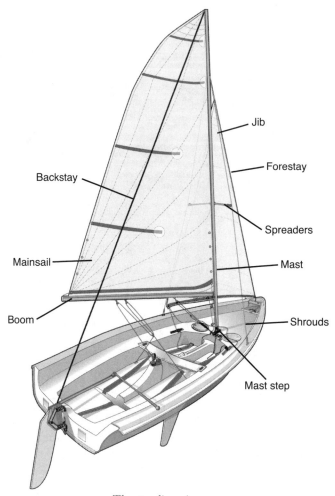

The standing rig.

The car analogy goes awry when you look up from the hull, because unlike cars, where there is nothing up there, sailboats have masts and *booms* and all sorts of wires and stuff. A boat's *standing rig* is the structure that supports the mast, while the *running rig* are the lines that control the sails. There are boats with more than one mast, as well as boats with freestanding masts without wires—but for simplicity's sake, we're just going to look at the most common set-up—a sloop rig with one mast and two sails.

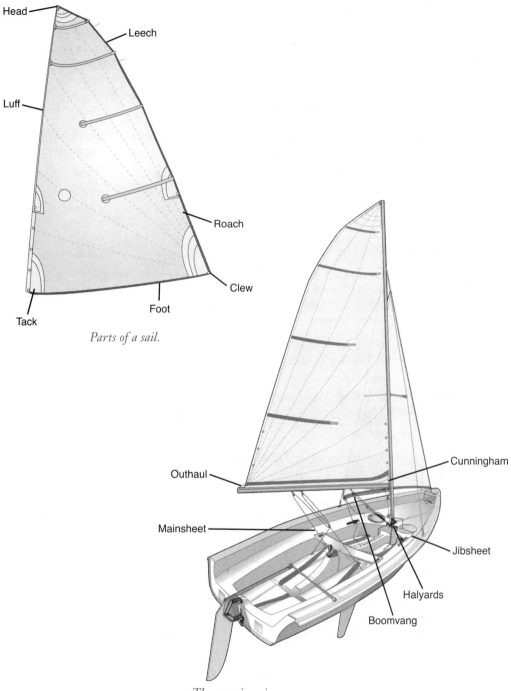

Head

Leech

Luff

Roach

Clew

Foot

Tack

Parts of a sail.

Outhaul

Cunningham

Mainsheet

Jibsheet

Halyards

Boomvang

The running rig.

Sails are what power a sailboat, but they only work when trimmed (adjusted) and controlled correctly. You might want to make a point of memorizing the terms that make up the running rig and then make a game of locating the mainsheet, jib sheets, and halyards on every boat you see—they can be set up quite differently.

Nautical Words and Commands

It should be enough to learn a bunch of new terms for boat parts—but for whatever reason, sailors also use nautical speak for describing the action on a boat. You don't go inside, you go through the *companionway* and *down below*. Rather than going a specific direction, you often steer the boat in relation to the wind—by *heading up* or *bearing off* and your speed is not measured in miles per hour—it is measured in *knots*.

> **DEFINITION**
>
> The nautical **knot** is the unit of speed for the boat, or wind that's equal to 1 nautical mile per hour (roughly 1.15 mph). The term is based on an early sailing tool called a chip log—which sailors used to measure boat speed by counting knots on a length of twine.
>
> Keep in mind when using the term, knot has a built-in meaning of "per hour." So you'd say you're traveling at 4 knots (not 4 knots per hour).

Here are a few of the more commonly used words and terms aboard. Don't feel like you need to memorize these in one sitting, and keep in mind some of the terminology is affected by regionalisms:

- *Abeam:* If you are looking for something abeam of you, you'd be looking out to the side.

- *Aft:* To find something aft of the boat, look astern or over the back of the boat (hopefully ahead is self-evident).

- *Bear off* or *bear away* or *fall off:* Turn the boat away from the wind.

- *Head up:* Steer closer to the wind.

- *Port:* Port is always the left-hand side of the boat when you're facing the bow. Using right and left can get confusing (whose left?), so port is always used to define the left-hand side of the boat in relation to the bow, or front. *See* starboard.

- *Starboard:* Starboard is always the right-hand side of the boat when you are facing the bow. *See* port.

- *Leeward:* Leeward is the direction opposite to the way the wind is currently blowing (windward). If you are feeling seasick, you'll want to visit the leeward side of the boat—because if you visit the windward side and it's windy, things can, umm, blow back.

- *Windward:* The direction from which the wind is currently blowing. If you sit facing out on the windward side of the boat, you'll feel wind on your face.

- *Tacking:* A sailing maneuver in which you turn the bow of the boat through the wind so that the wind changes from one side of the boat to the other side.

- *Jibing:* The opposite of tacking, this maneuver refers to turning the stern of the boat through the wind so that the wind changes from one side of the boat to the other side.

Finding a Ride

Now that you have the lingo down and a general idea of a few commands, you might be thinking about catching a ride and seeing how it all works. One way to get out on the water is to check with friends who have boats and ask to tag along on a day cruise, while another way is to sign up as crew for beer-can races at a local yacht club. (These short races are run in protected waters during the mild summer season.)

If you don't feel ready just to jump on a boat, consider taking lessons. Actually, consider taking lessons anyway, because they really are the best way to learn to sail safely.

Most U.S. sailing schools offer a curriculum designed by either the United States Sailing Association ("US Sailing") or the American Sailing Association (ASA). The courses are similar, but different schools have different approaches, so call around. To find a school near you, visit sailingcertification.com for US Sailing schools or asa.com/find_a_sailing_school.html for ASA schools.

BETTER BOATING

Keep these key points in mind when packing for a day on the water.

- Wear soft-soled, nonmarking shoes.
- Bring a hat, sunglasses, and sunscreen.
- It's often cooler on the water, so bring an extra layer.
- Pack a windbreaker or raincoat if rain is forecast. And if you are prone to motion sickness, bring your medication.

Learn to Sail by Chartering

Charter holidays aren't just for skilled sailors—many companies also offer a range of live-aboard courses that give novice sailors the opportunity to learn basic sailing skills while introducing them to the nuts and bolts of boat ownership.

Charter holidays can be more than an opportunity to sail in beautiful tropical waters with friends and family—they can also be an opportunity to develop sailing skills.
(Evan Gatehouse)

Charter companies are found worldwide (some are bigger, better, or more reputable than others), but most can be researched on internet sites. Pay careful attention to the actual location of the fleet and the condition of the boats available. Other factors in choosing a company include whether you want a crewed charter (in which a paid crew does most of the work but you can chip in as much as you like) or a full charter-and-learn course that leads to certification.

Many sailors prefer just to charter boats rather than own one because it's kind of a best-of-all-worlds scenario—you get to sail in a gorgeous place but if something wears out or breaks down, you don't need to foot the bill to fix it. Another benefit of chartering is if you are thinking of buying a specific type of boat, you can charter one, or something similar, before taking the plunge.

BETTER BOATING

Many people rule out boating forever after a bout with *mal de mer,* or seasickness. But in reality many long-time sailors regularly suffer through the dizziness, nausea, shakes, and occasional vomiting, moderating the symptoms with both experience and medication. If you think you may be prone to seasickness, avoid alcohol, caffeine, and spicy or heavy foods before your sail. If symptoms start, sit in the fresh air, facing the direction of travel in a seat where you'll experience the least motion (typically as close to the mast as possible). Keep your gaze on the horizon and consider taking seasickness medication or sipping ginger ale and munching crackers.

Racing as Apprentice Crew

Another great way to get time on the water is by joining a boat for race nights at your local yacht club or marina. All those sheets, sails, halyards, and winches are easier to run with crew, so most boat owners heading out on a sail have room for an extra body or two. Especially if the crew in question can distinguish the mainsail from the jib. (The mainsail is the big one that's attached to the mast and boom; the jib, or genoa, is the foresail found at the front of the boat.)

Race boats require a large crew to run them, and many boats have room on harbor races for a novice crew who is eager to learn more.
(Diane Selkirk)

Once you're aboard, make sure you're kitted out with safety gear (Personal Floatation Device [PFD] and a harness if conditions warrant) and are oriented to the boat. Most skippers will show new boaters where the *head* is (bathroom), where to store your gear, where additional safety equipment is located, and how to use the VHF radio's safety features. You should also be shown how the cockpit is arranged and told what your job will be.

SAILOR'S WARNING

If you plan to sail more than once or twice, you should purchase your own PFD. They are called *personal* floatation devices because individual life vests fit differently and have varied uses.

The key is to choose a lifejacket you'll wear; it could save your life. Statistics show most drowning victims owned PFDs but weren't wearing them.

Although being a novice means you won't be expected to do much, it does help to have some idea about what everyone is doing. Typically on a race boat of 30 feet or so you'll have a combination of these positions:

- *Helmsman/Skipper:* The person who drives the boat and calls out commands
- *Tactician:* Uses the wind, currents, and conditions to find the most favorable course
- *Main trimmer:* Adjusts the sheets that control the mainsail
- *Port Trimmer:* Controls the foresail and the spinnaker
- *Starboard Trimmer:* Controls the foresail and the spinnaker
- *Pitman (or Pit):* Works with the bowman (or foredeck crew) and stows sails below deck
- *Bowman:* Gets the spinnaker ready to deploy and to retrieve and makes sure everything runs smoothly on the bow

Then there is the *rail meat*. Rail meat are those crew members in a race who scramble from one high side of the boat to another to balance the boat. It's often your first job if you're new to sailing, but any crew member who's not actively working will join you on the rail.

While it sounds simple, you do have to plan your route across the deck—keeping an eye out for trimmers and moving lines and then positioning yourself correctly on deck (legs over the side, harness clipped on if it's rough). Once you're in place, enjoy the ride—but also keep an eye on what's happening around you. Things can move quickly and there's a lot to learn.

Boats and Their Infinite Variety

Walk down a busy dock in a large marina and you'll notice the myriad ways sailboat design can differ one from the next. Some differences will be obvious—like the variations in length and width, and the number of masts and hulls. But then there are the more subtle distinctions between stern shape, freeboard (the height of the hull above the water), cockpit placement and size, bow shape, cabin configuration, and even the materials the boat is made from. If you could peek underwater, you'd see differences in hull shape, keel configuration, and the size and design of the rudder.

Generally sailboats are described according to their hull configuration (monohull, catamaran, trimaran), keel type (full, fin, wing, bulb, water ballast, etc.), purpose (leisure, racing, cruising), number and arrangement of masts (sloop, yawl, schooner, etc.) or sail plan (fractional rig, cutter, junk, etc.).

Many factors contribute to the different designs of sailboats. But the basic goal is to pair the sails and the hull(s) to provide a certain type of performance for the sailor.

Common Boats for New Sailors

The most common boats a newer sailor might be interested in include dinghies, sailers, cruisers, and catamarans. Each boat has a different purpose and suits a different number of people.

Small sailing dinghy.
(Evan Gatehouse)

Large sailing dinghy.
(Evan Gatehouse)

Trailer sailer.
(Catalina Yachts)

Small dinghies are perfect first boats for kids learning to sail and hoping to go on to race. They fit between one adult and child to up to three kids.

Larger dinghies are great for day sailing in *sheltered waters* and will fit two adults.

Trailer sailers are compact sailboats that are small enough to tow on a trailer but are still large enough to accommodate two or more—which makes them great for day or weekend sailing.

DEFINITION

Sheltered waters includes bays, inlets, and harbors that are protected from high winds and rough waves in most weather conditions. Sheltered waters are also defined as waterways where sailors can easily get to safety should weather conditions deteriorate.

Traditional cruiser.
(Evan Gatehouse)

Traditional full-keeled cruising boats have a different shape than more modern boats—they are narrower across the beam and may have more than one mast and typically fit up to four in comfort. Because of their age, they often make an affordable first boat.

Production cruisers make up the bulk of new sailboats on the market. Typically sloop rigged with a wide beam and stern, their roomy interior makes them popular with families of four and for entertaining groups up to six.

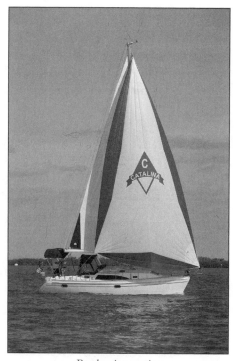

Production cruiser.
(Catalina Yachts)

Designed for the cruiser who wants to race or the racer who wants to cruise, racer-cruisers will have the comforts of a production cruising boat but in a lighter, stronger design. Small racer-cruisers are designed to be raced by crews of two to six.

Racer-cruiser.
(Evan Gatehouse)

Multihull.
(Evan Gatehouse)

The number of production catamarans available worldwide shows they are ever increasing in popularity. Like monohulls, multihulls come in trailerable, production cruiser, racer-cruiser, and blue water designs.

The Least You Need to Know

- The language of sailing is specific and a bit archaic, but essential to learn if you want to understand what's happening on the water.
- Going sailing with an experienced boater and joining a race boat for an evening race are great ways to get a feel for sailing, but taking lessons is the best way to learn.
- Being prone to seasickness doesn't rule out sailing—many long-time sailors get ill but have learned strategies to manage their symptoms.
- Boats come in all shapes and sizes—and each type has a specific purpose. Some sailboats make better starter boats than others.

Weather and Whatnot

In This Chapter

- Weather forecasts, and whether to go sailing
- Knowing where the wind is coming from
- Learning how the wind makes a boat sail
- Understanding apparent and true wind

One of the most important skills I've developed as a sailor is an understanding of the weather. When I first sailed, I'd check the weather report and believe it. It was always a shock when conditions weren't quite as advertised, or the wind shifted direction before it was forecast to, or a rain shower hit seemingly without warning.

Over time, though, I've discovered that checking the report is simply the first step in weather awareness. These days I'll check the report, compare what I've discovered to actual on-the-water conditions, and then keep a careful eye on the sky, the waves, and the wind direction so I'm aware of potential changes before they even occur.

This way I'm not surprised by an afternoon thunderstorm—because I've noted the building clouds. And I'm not caught out by a shift in wind direction because I saw the change in the clouds and wave pattern that signaled its approach.

Making Sense of the Weather

Weather determines where we can sail, when we can sail there, and if we should actually be sailing at all. But if your typical weather check includes little more than noting the day's temperature range and checking whether or not you'll need an umbrella—it's time to look a little deeper.

SAILOR'S WARNING

The U.S. Coast Guard's "Recreational Boating Statistics" lists boating in poor weather or hazardous waters as one of the primary causes of boating accidents. Boaters head out on what looks like a nice day only to have conditions deteriorate and become unsafe.

A marine weather report can tell us sailors a lot more than if it's a good day for a barbeque. Of course knowing the temperature is handy, and it's nice to know whether to expect sun or rain, but your big focus should be on the wind—you need to know wind speed, wind direction, if the wind is building or decreasing in strength, or if it's changing in direction.

The wind is your biggest concern—not just because too much can be dangerous and too little is a bit boring. Wind also influences the *sea state*, by creating waves, choppy seas, ripples, or *swells*.

DEFINITION

Sea state is a fancy phrase for describing what the surface of the ocean looks like. It describes the size of waves, how rough they are, and whether or not there is a current.

Swells vary from wind waves in that they tend to be generated a long way from where you encounter them and roll steadily across a body of water. Wind waves are generated by local conditions, so they start soon after the wind blows and end shortly after the wind stops. A swell keeps on rolling, and an area may experience very large swells from a storm that occurred hundreds of miles away.

Where to Get the Weather

There are plenty of places to get weather forecasts from, but not all of them focus on marine forecasts. So whether you get your weather from the Weather Channel, which typically gives regular local updates as well as bigger picture stuff, websites that specialize in general weather such as Weather Underground (www.wunderground. com), or sailor-oriented sites like Passage Weather (passageweather.com), you need to be sure you're getting information that tells you everything you should know.

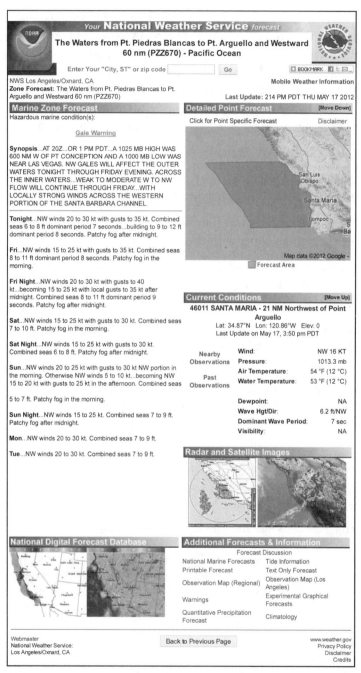

NOAA marine forecasts are presented a bit differently than regular forecasts and tend to focus on a very specific geographical area and include current conditions, a forecast, and links to radar and satellite images.

(Courtesy NOAA)

One of the more useful sources of marine weather is the National Oceanic and Atmospheric Administration (NOAA). The NOAA's reports can be found online (nws. noaa.gov/om/marine/home.htm)—though the NOAA does not advise using the website for weather reports because these online forecasts can be out of date. Most people tune in by listening to NOAA Weather Radio on their boat's VHF radio (press WX-1, WX-2, or WX-3). Keep in mind you can also get the NOAA's forecasts in advance by requesting weather reports by email, or setting up text messages for your phone.

Specific parts of an NOAA forecast:

- Advisories and warnings: The forecast will mention any warnings for extreme weather or hazards in your area (from Small Craft Warning to Hurricane).

- Synopsis: This gives you the "big picture," describing weather systems all over the region, along with their directions and intensity.

- Area forecast: You'll get the predicted weather for your specific area including wind speed in knots, its direction, wind wave height, swell direction, and the outlook for the next several days.

- Current conditions: These will be given for a specific geographic point and help you judge if the weather report and real-life conditions are matching up.

The NOAA's forecasts are pretty accurate, but the timing and intensity of the weather can be off. And keep in mind the forecasts cover large areas, so learning the locations that are referenced can be helpful.

NAUTICAL KNOWLEDGE

Ever wondered about the old adage, "Red sky at night, sailor's delight. Red sky in morning, sailor's warning"?

It turns out to be true. When the sky glows red at sunset, the color is caused by sun shining through a high concentration of dust particles—indicating stable air coming in from the west. Basically good weather will follow. But a red sunrise indicates that a storm system may be moving to the east. The more vivid the red, the more likely it is that rain is on its way.

Weather Words

The first time you read or listen to a marine forecast you might wonder what the heck they're even talking about. So it's a good idea to listen to a few of them and learn the lingo before relying on one.

Some of the words and phrases you might read or hear pretty much mean stay home, or if you're on the water they mean get to safety pronto:

- *Small Craft:* Just so you know there's no formal definition of a small craft (though informally it often refers to boats under 33 ft. in length). Generally, the term is used for boaters who are operating smaller boats in conditions that are rougher than they have experience with.

- *Small Craft Advisory* (SCA): The conditions that trigger a small craft advisory vary, but in most areas this means winds of 22 to 33 knots (25–38 m.p.h.) and matching hazardous seas.

- *Small Craft Advisory* for Rough Bar (SCARB): An advisory for harbor or river entrances known as bars. Waves over a bar can be especially dangerous during certain conditions.

- *Gale Warning:* This announcement warns of winds of 34 to 47 knots (39–54 m.p.h.).

- *Storm Warning:* Winds of 48 to 63 knots (55–73 m.p.h.).

- *Tropical Storm Warning:* An announcement that tropical storm conditions with winds of 34 to 63 knots (39– 73 m.p.h.) are coming.

- *Hurricane Warning:* Hurricane conditions with sustained winds of 63 knots (73 m.p.h.) or higher are coming.

- *Special Marine Warning* (SMW): These nonscheduled forecasts warn of sudden events (think thunderstorms, hail, or waterspouts) that are short-lived but potentially dangerous.

NAUTICAL KNOWLEDGE

What's the difference between Advisories, Watches, and Warnings for Marine Areas?

- Advisory: A significant weather event (think hurricane, flooding, hazardous seas, large surf, etc.) is possible in your area.
- Watch: The weather event is not only likely, it will have a serious impact.
- Warning: A serious weather event that threatens life and property is occurring, imminent, or highly likely.

Reading the Sky

Once you've been out sailing in the same location a few times, you'll realize that while weather forecasts are pretty accurate, they often don't account for more subtle *local conditions* that happen through the day. If you were to ask long-time sailors, most would tell you about things like predictable wind direction changes, increases in the afternoon breeze, or well-known wind effects (often with their own names like *Nor'easter, Diablo, Sundowner, or Chinook*) that happen during specific weather patterns.

It can take time and experience to learn about these regional weather patterns, but it's never too soon to start trusting your eyes. If conditions are changing on the water or the sky is looking different, pay attention. Things can happen quickly.

NAUTICAL KNOWLEDGE

Mare's tails and mackerel scales, soon will be time to shorten sails.

—Old sailor's proverb

One telltale sign of change is the look of the clouds. Here are six types of clouds and what they signify:

- Cirrus clouds are often called "mare's tails" due to their wispy appearance. Made of ice crystals, they signal a weather change.

- Altocumulus clouds are small clumpy clouds resembling fish scales in the sky that often precede cold fronts.

- Cirrostratus clouds are also made of ice crystals. Forming thin veil-like layers, they may be a sign that rain is on its way.

- Cumulus clouds are fluffy white clouds that commonly indicate fine sailing weather. However, if clouds get bigger and darker, thunderstorms may develop.

- Cirrocumulus clouds are thin white wisps with a hint of fluffy white. Cirrocumulus clouds are a sign of fine sailing weather to come.

- Cumulonimbus clouds form from cumulus clouds and are usually a sign that squalls are approaching. Squalls often bring gusty winds, heavy rain, and potentially, thunder and lightning.

Cumulus clouds.
(Courtesy NOAA)

Cumulonimbus clouds.
(Courtesy NOAA)

Working with the Wind

A while back we went for a wonderful sail—the wind was out of the southeast, which meant we sailed on a leisurely *broad reach*. A few hours after we anchored at our destination, another sailor who made the same passage leaving at the same time arrived. But he complained that the northwest winds had been impossible and no matter how he adjusted his sails for *close reaching* his boat barely moved.

> **DEFINITION**
>
> When a boat is on a **broad reach** the wind is coming over the stern slightly off to one side and blowing into the sail from behind—pushing your boat along.
>
> **Close reaching** is when the wind comes over the bow and slightly to one side. The sails are in fairly tight and using the foil shape of the sails your boat is pulled along.

It turned out that he was a novice sailor who was confused about wind direction. He didn't realize that the wind is named after the direction it comes from (so a west wind blows from the west to the east—it doesn't blow to the west). The real problem, though, was that in misnaming the wind, he also misunderstood how to properly set his sails. (Okay, so the whole thing was a problem—new sailors really shouldn't set out alone.)

Sailors talk about the wind with such reverence it's almost as if we believe the wind-god brothers Boreas, Zephyrus, Eurus, and Nortus are out there huffing and puffing up the gusts. But understanding the direction and strength of a breeze really is essential. If you don't know where the wind is coming from, no other part of sailing is going to make much sense, and it's going to be really tricky to get to where you're going.

Wind Direction: Figuring It Out

Knowing that the forecast is for an easterly wind isn't quite the same as understanding where the wind is coming from. To do that, you have to learn to feel the wind. Head outside to an open space and turn until you face the wind. After a couple of tries it should be obvious—you'll feel it move evenly across your cheeks and hear the same level of sound in each ear. Now look around: flags fluttering (they stream away from the wind), trees bending, smoke drifting through the air—they all show you the wind direction.

Wind indicators like this Windex have an arrow that points toward the direction the wind is coming from.
(Courtesy Windex)

Aboard a sailboat, we have even more tools. Dinghies will commonly have *telltales*, short pieces of yarn that are tied to the shrouds, while larger boats often will have flags or burgees as well as a masthead wind indicator at the top of the mast that has an arrow which points into the wind. On the water you can also keep an eye out for sails on other boats (if they're set correctly) and ripples across the water. Larger waves and swells, however, can be deceptive—they're often generated hours before you see them, by forces that may have since changed.

The Beaufort Scale

Wondering how windy it is? In 1806, Rear-Admiral Sir Francis Beaufort did the sailing world a favor by developing a table that classified wind by strength and how it appeared to the sailor. The table worked so well it's still in use today.

Beaufort Number	Knots	Wind Description	Sea State	Effect of Wind on Boats 15–40 Ft.
Force 0	< 1	Calm	Sea smooth and glassy	Becalmed
Force 1	1–3	Light air	Rippled surface ruffled by wind; some smooth patches	Sails loosely filled
Force 2	4–6	Light breeze	Entire surface ruffled; small waves with glassy crests	Sails filled
Force 3	7–10	Gentle breeze	Large wavelets; occasional white caps	Sails filled boat heels.
Force 4	11–16	Moderate breeze	Small waves; half the waves show whitecaps	Small boats reefed
Force 5	17–21	Fresh breeze	Moderate waves; most crests show whitecaps; some spray	Small boats reefed; larger boats shorten sail
Force 6	22–27	Strong breeze	Large waves; whitecaps everywhere; foam and spray	Small boats return to port; larger craft double reefed

Beaufort Number	Knots	Wind Description	Sea State	Effect of Wind on Boats 15–40 Ft.
Force 7	28–33	Moderate gale	Sea heaps up, spray, breaking waves	Most boats seek shelter
Force 8	34–40	Fresh gale	Moderately high waves; streaks of foam	Boats that cannot reach shelter sail with great care
Force 9	41–47	Strong gale	High waves; dense streaks of foam; spray may affect visibility	Sail with great care
Force 10	48–55	Whole gale	Very high waves; great foam patches; much spray	Sail with great care

Working with the wind involves more than knowing wind strength (and understanding how it may affect the sea state) and sailing conditions (and the way you adjust your sails). Knowing where the wind is coming from will help you decide how you are going to set your sails and determine which point of sail you are on.

Points of Sail: How the Wind Moves Your Boat

While many sailboats do have an engine, the general goal of owning a sailboat is to sail places. This means you'll need to understand how the wind moves your boat. When you take a sailing course, a good portion of the classroom time is dedicated to understanding the points of sailing (or "points of sail")—the angle the wind hits the sails at and what the corresponding sail shape should be.

Points of Sail

Wind direction

Close reach

The wind is coming from somewhere between Close Hauled and a Beam Reach. Sails are slightly eased and the centerboard is ¾ down.

Close hauled

The boat is sailing as close to the wind as possible. Sails are pulled in tight and the centerboard is fully down.

Head-to-wind

The wind is coming over the bow and hitting both sides of your sails equally. This is the no-sail zone.

Downwind run

Broad reach

The wind is coming over the stern. The sails are all the way out and may be wing on wing with the main on one side and the jib on the other. The centerboard is almost all the way up.

Beam reach

The wind is coming over the beam at about a 90 degree angle. Sails are eased partway out and the centerboard is ¹/₂-way down.

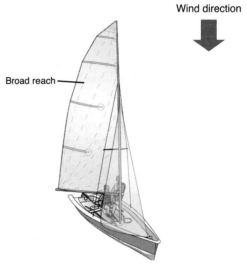

Wind direction

Broad reach

The wind is coming over the stern quarter. Sails are eased much of the way out and the centerboard is ³/₄ of the way up.

Beam reach

Close hauled

Close reach

Points of sail tends to be one of those things that make no sense and then suddenly, it all comes together. So I'll cover the topic in two ways. In this chapter, I discuss how wind moves your boat. In Chapter 5, I'll cover what your role is with steering and sail shape.

First off, points of sail includes the terms used to describe the direction your boat is sailing in relation to the wind. If you're sailing "close to the wind," your bow is pointing upwind and the breeze is hitting near the front of your boat first. *Reaching* means your bow is angling away from the wind and the wind hits near the middle of the boat first. *Sailing downwind* means the wind hits the stern first.

Sailing downwind or running is easy to understand: the wind blows into your sails, pushes against them, and moves your boat. You can understand what's happening if you blow something light across the table—it only works if you're behind the object. What this means for your boat is the more area of sail you have out to catch the wind, the faster you'll go. But when going downwind on a typical boat with normal sails, you'll never sail faster than the wind.

Sailing directly upwind is also easy to understand: you can't do it. Your boat will simply sit there with its sails flapping and you'll probably start to drift backward. What's happening is the wind is blowing equally on both sides of the sail, which makes your sails into big flags and puts you *in irons* or *head-to-wind.* This tends to happen a lot when people are learning to sail—and the goal when it occurs is to maneuver the boat to get the wind back in the right place.

In most other points of sail, from close-hauled (where the wind is coming from pretty close to the front of the boat and the sails are hauled in tight) to broad reaching (the wind coming from close to astern and the sails reach way out), the wind will split and go around both sides of the sail. If you have the sails set correctly, areas of low and high pressure will be created. This is where the aerodynamics part of sailing comes in. Sails have curvature, like airplane wings, and the different areas of air pressure create *lift*, pulling the boat forward.

NAUTICAL KNOWLEDGE

Wind never stays steady—it's constantly shifting in speed and direction. As a sailor you need to pay attention to the changes. Keep an eye on the surface of the water upwind of you—dark ruffled patches called *cat's paws* indicate a gust is coming while smooth glassy areas show that you may be sailing into a *lull,* or an area of light wind.

True Versus Apparent Wind

Apparent wind is one of those concepts that confuses even long-time sailors. Simply put, it's the combination of two winds: the *true wind* (the one nature made), and the one your boat creates when it's in motion.

The clearest way I've heard apparent wind explained (I've had it explained in lots of unclear ways, too) is this: stand still. That breeze you feel is the true wind. Now run into the wind. That increase in wind you feel is the apparent wind. It's the wind you've created by running plus the wind that is blowing. If you were to run down-wind away from the breeze, the apparent wind you would feel would diminish.

Apparent wind matters for a couple of reasons. The most important to new sailors is about simple safety. Let's say you're sailing at 6 knots in a 14-knot breeze. If you're going downwind, the apparent wind is the true wind minus your boat speed, or 8 knots. That's not much wind, so the forces on your sails aren't much. But if you were to go upwind, say close-hauled, the apparent wind would be added to the true wind and become 22 knots, which means there is a lot more force on your sails and it may be time to *reef* or reduce your sail area.

As you gain experience, understanding apparent wind will affect how you *trim* or adjust your sails, or your course—especially in gusty conditions. If you are sailing upwind and the true wind increases in a gust, the apparent wind is going to shift aft (just trust me on this). So to stay properly trimmed you'll need to head up in the gust and bear back off in the lull.

The Least You Need to Know

- It's essential to get a weather report before heading out on the water, and it's preferable to get a marine forecast.
- You should learn about common local weather conditions and how to interpret changes in cloud cover.
- Learning where the wind is coming from takes practice, but understanding its origin will make you a better sailor.
- Learning the points of sail helps you describe your boat's course in relation to the wind direction.
- There are two types of wind in sailing—true wind and apparent wind—and it's important to learn the difference between them.

Tides, Currents, and You

In This Chapter

- Understanding tides and currents
- Reading tide tables
- Determining currents
- Navigating tips for tides and currents

There's nothing quite so frustrating (and potentially embarrassing) as forgetting to check the tides and currents and discovering the hard way that a 3-knot current moves you at exactly the same rate as the forecasted light breeze (which you knew about because you checked the weather).

In case you can't picture this, visualize a sailboat with its sails filled with wind, its crew eager to get somewhere, but the boat not actually moving because the boat's forward speed and current have cancelled each other out.

It gets even worse when the breeze dies a bit and you start to float backward—away from your intended destination. The only thing that might make this scenario worse is when you discover that a local wreck (which is normally way underwater) is now exposed because of the *spring tides*, and you are about to drift right into it.

True story.

Making Sense of Tides and Currents

Somewhere back in elementary school you probably learned that tides are generated by a combination of gravitational forces caused by the moon, the sun, and the rotation of the earth. Since then, if you've walked the beach now and again, you've probably paid enough attention to know most places experience two high tides and two low tides each day (semidiurnal), and that tidal ranges can vary from negligible to more than 20 feet. Beyond that, the tides may not have seemed very important.

But to sailors, tides can be just as important as wind. Depending on where you are sailing, the tides (the vertical movement of water) can have a major effect on your plans. Not only does a fluctuating tide dramatically alter the seascape (in some locations a low tide may look very different than high tide as underwater hazards, reefs, or rocks come into striking range), but they can also create currents (the horizontal movement of water).

As you might imagine, if you have a tidal range of 12 feet or so (as in the Puget Sound) all that water going up and down is going to generate a lot of motion—especially at the mouths of harbors or anyplace the water's movement is restricted.

Tidal Words

The movement of water comes with its own set of terms. You can certainly say the tide goes in and out, or up and down, but knowing the specific language does make it easier to understand why the tide may be higher from one hour to the next. Here are some terms to know:

- *Tidal range:* The distance between the highest water level during a high tide and the lowest water level during a low tide.

- *Spring tides:* Have nothing to do with spring; occur every full and new moon and have the largest tidal range.

- *Neap tides:* The smallest tides; occur during the first and last quarters of the moon.

- *Ebb tide:* Water going down toward low tide.

- *Flood tide:* Water rising toward a high tide.

- *Slack Water:* Times when the water movement or current is minimal. Because of the time it takes for bays and estuaries to drain out, slack water is not necessarily at high tide and low tide.

Learning to Predict the Tides

Before you set sail, you'll need to make yourself familiar with the tides in your area. If you're using a chart plotter and electronic charts, it's often a simple matter of selecting the place you want to see the tide for and choosing the day. If you don't have a chart plotter and are just heading out for a short daysail, you can find basic tidal information in your daily newspaper, online at tidesandcurrents.noaa.gov, or on some weather forecasts.

However, if you are going to be sailing regularly, it's not a bad idea to pick up a *tide table* for your cruising area. Keep in mind the tables are published every year, so make sure the table you're using is current.

Using a Tide Table

Tide tables typically include data in two forms: a printed table and a graphic chart. Both have the same basic information, but reading them is a bit different.

A typical tide table might look like this:

Station Name: SOUTH BEACH, YAQUINA RIVER, OR

From: 2012/05/18 12:00 A.M.–2012/05/19 11:59 P.M.

Units: Feet

Time Zone: LST/LDT

Datum: MLLW

Interval Type: High/Low Tide Predictions

Date	Day	Time	Pred	High/Low
2012/05/18	Fri	05:43 A.M.	−0.07	L
2012/05/18	Fri	12:14 P.M.	6.4	H
2012/05/18	Fri	05:25 P.M.	2.67	L
2012/05/18	Fri	11:34 P.M.	8.23	H
2012/05/19	Sat	06:19 A.M.	−0.46	L

The first thing you might notice is tide tables are for a specific location. Tides can vary quite a bit from one place to the next, so finding a tidal station that's as close as possible to where you'll be sailing means you're less likely to run aground.

The next detail that often surprises people is that even though there are four tides daily, they're not on an exact 6-hour schedule. In fact, the period between tide cycles is roughly 13 hours from high to high or low to low.

The next detail you need to note is the *datum*—the level of water that depths are measured from. On this table the datum is mean lower low water (MLLW), which means tide heights are measured from the lowest average tide at this station.

Reading a table beyond that is just a matter of practice. In this example, the first low tide of the day is -0.07 at 05:43 A.M. (this means the tide is .07 ft. below an average low tide) and it floods until 12:14 P.M. At 12:14 the tide will be 6.4 feet. Then the tide ebbs until 5:25 P.M. to 2.67 feet.

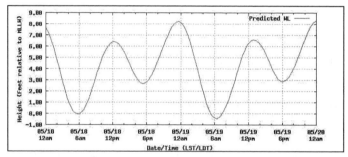

A tidal chart is less precise than a table, but seeing the tide in a graphic form can make it easier to understand the movement of the water.

(Courtesy NOAA)

The graphics on tidal charts give the same info as the table—they just do it by way of a wavy line. The high part of the line shows high tide; the lowest part on the line is low tide. The graphic makes it easy to see that not all tides are the same in a day; typically two tide cycles will be smaller. In this case, the 12:14 P.M. to 5:25 P.M. tide has a range of less than 4 feet while the 11:34 P.M. to 6:19 A.M. tide has a range of over 8 feet.

BETTER BOATING

When anchoring, you need to know how much the tide may change from the moment you arrive to when you leave. In some areas the tidal range may be so small you can easily guess the changing depth. But in places with a large tidal range, anchoring in too shallow an area means you could hit the bottom, and choosing too deep a spot means you may not have enough anchor line out to stay attached to the bottom.

The key is to work out how much the tide will rise and fall between the time that you anchor and when you leave. With our example, if you arrive around 1:00 P.M. on Friday, the tide is going to first fall roughly 6 feet and then rise roughly 2 feet during the next 24 hours.

Understanding Currents

If tide is the rise and fall of the water, and current is the flow, then you might assume current would be slack at low tide and high tides, and run at its fastest rate in the middle of the time between high and low. And in some cases this is true. Mostly, though, not so much.

If you were to make your way up a river like the Hudson, or through the estuaries in San Francisco Bay, or up through Alaska's Inside Passage, you would likely notice some pretty significant differences between when high tide is listed on a tide table and when the current actually starts to ebb. In areas of large tides and strong currents, many factors influence the currents, from the shape of land mass, to the depth of the water, to recent wind storms or, on rivers, heavy rains. The result is currents are not easily predicted, which is why many locations have *current tables*.

Valuable hints about the state of the current can come from buoys, anchored boats, and drifting objects. Buoys may lean with the current, showing both a bow wave and a trail of disturbed water and bubbles that stream in the direction of flow.
(Evan Gatehouse)

Like tide tables, current tables change every year, and even more so than tide tables, current tables are only a prediction. This is especially important to know when planning to sail through narrow passages or entering a river bar, since the currents can be very dangerous and strong.

The entrance to a river (and some harbors) often has patches of shallow water or sandbars, and when an incoming or outgoing tide hits this shallow region it can result in large waves and turbulent water. Conditions are worst when you have wind blowing in one direction and the tide going in the other; conditions are best during periods of slack water.

Reading a Current Table

Current tables are typically found in text form at tidesandcurrents.noaa.gov and are for a specific location, often the opening to a channel, a narrows, or the opening to a bay. The typical rule of thumb is to travel through an area of current at slack water, or as close to slack water as you can manage.

Here is a partial example of a current table for Deception Pass:

Deception Pass Predicted Tidal Current
June 1, 2012
Flood (+) Direction, True.
Ebb (–) Direction, True.

Slack Water	Maximum Current		Slack Water	Maximum Current		Slack Water
Time	*Time*	*Velocity*	*Time*	*Time*	*Velocity*	*Time*
0041	0400		0728	1035		1409
	–7.4 knots			+6.2 knots		

This partial current table is simplified to show three periods of slack water (12:41 A.M., 7:28 A.M., and 2:09 P.M.), one ebb current (7.4 knots at 4:00 A.M.) and one flood current (6.2 knots at 10:35 am). Boats wanting to travel through this pass would likely make their way through during the daylight slack water times.

Navigating in Tidal Currents

Tidal currents have two important components: their direction and their speed. And because they're linked to the rising and falling of tide, the speed varies and the direction reverses.

NAUTICAL KNOWLEDGE

Keep in mind, the direction or set of a current is defined by the direction it's traveling, unlike wind, which is defined by the direction it comes from.

On charts and tables, a flood current is shown as a positive number (+) and the ebb current is shown as a negative (–).

In a perfect world you simply time it so you are going wherever the current is going, whenever it's going there. This way you'll be fast and may save money on motoring. *Perfect* is a term that rarely applies to sailing, though, and it's more likely that you'll need to make some sort of allowance for adverse current at some point in your sailing adventures.

Things to keep in mind about currents when you're on the water:

- Tidal currents typically flow the fastest in the deepest part of a channel and slowest in the shallow patches.

- If you are trying to sail against the current, stick to the edges of a channel or close to shore.

- Heavy boats with more hull underwater are more affected by the tide than lighter boats with less underwater structure. So a heavy full-keeled boat will be more affected than a centre-board dinghy.

- Wind blowing the same direction the tide is running can push the water and speed up the current beyond its predicted strength.

- When the wind is opposing the tide, short steep waves can be produced. In strong winds and strong currents these seas can create dangerous conditions.

- If your boat makes 5 knots under sail or power and the current is running against you at 5 knots, you are not going to make any progress.

- If your boat makes 5 knots and the current is running against you at 3 knots and you have 10 nautical miles to go, simple math says it's going to take 5 hours to get there, no matter how long it took last time.

Getting There from Here

Navigating can get trickier when you're sailing *across* a current. Simply put, you might think you're going one way, but the push from the current may be setting you a different direction. One way to check how badly the current is affecting your course is to steer your boat directly toward your destination and line up two objects (one in front of the other) to use as a range. An official range tends to be two navigation markers, but you can line up a tree and a house, a dock and a building, and so on.

Once you have your range, sail straight and then check your progress every so often. If you're drifting sideways with the current, the two objects will slip out of alignment and you'll need to adjust your course.

The Least You Need to Know

- Tides are the rise and fall of the water, and current is the flow.
- Tide tables give information about low and high tides for specific locations on specific days.
- Current tables provide information about the speed and direction of a current.
- Knowing the time and height of high and low tides and the speed and direction of currents is essential to safe navigation.

Basic Boat Handling

The goal is not to sail the boat, but rather to help the boat sail herself.

—John Rousmaniere, Author and Sailor

When you flip to Part 2, it's probably because sailing is starting to make sense and you're ready to climb aboard a boat. You understand some of the language and you realize now why sailboats never seem to go directly to their destination but instead seem to meander across the water.

In this part of the book you learn to rig and hoist your sails and then how to steer through the points of sail. You know what "tack" means now and can be ready to try tacking and then jibing as you make your way to your destination. You also learn a bit about using the motor and why steering a boat is quite different from driving a car. I also go through the steps involved in some of the more advanced beginner skills— anchoring, reducing sail, managing in bad weather, and getting a tow.

And I cover safety—because no matter how fun sailing is, there are still real risks involved, and learning to be safe is a high priority. So I cover when to call for help and what situations you can safely handle yourself, including running aground, engine troubles, and man overboard.

Basic Sailing Skills

In This Chapter

- Rigging and hoisting your sails
- Steering through the points of sail
- Using sail controls for trimming sails
- Tacking and jibing to your destination
- Reefing your sails and heaving to
- Righting a capsize

When I first learned to sail, I recall being told to pull in the jib sheet—*hard!*—which I did with all my might, until I had made the sail fantastically taut, and was suffused with pride over my skill at sail tightening. But then, rather than getting the praise I was sure I deserved, I was told to ease the sheet back out again. I recall thinking that sailing was a confounding activity that hurt my hands.

Frustrated, I mentioned this to my instructor. He patiently went over points of sail and sail trim, again, then in response to my blank look he guided my hands until the sail filled and I felt the boat respond. "Boats," he said, "tell you when the sails are set right. The theory behind 'points of sail' and sail trim is just a way of articulating that."

So keep that idea in mind as you read through this chapter. Consider points of sail as a guideline that gives words to something that's fundamentally a little magical. After you've sailed a few times, setting the sails will be less about trying to memorize what the diagrams say and more about responding to what the boat needs.

Raising the Sails

Going sailing means you need your sails up. But the tricky bit is as soon as your sails are raised, wind is going to blow on them. So before you hoist them you need to point the bow of the boat directly into the wind so the wind acts on both sides of the sails evenly and they luff, or flap in the breeze the way a flag does.

Typically sails are raised in the same order. The main, as the boat's most powerful sail, is raised first. Then the foresail, known as a jib or genoa, is raised second.

SAILOR'S WARNING

No two sailboats are rigged the same. Even the same model of boat will often have differences in how the sails are attached, where lines are led, and how the trim controls are set up. Before raising the sails on any new boat, be sure to orient yourself to how that boat is laid out.

Preparing the Main for Sailing

Depending on the boat, the mainsail may be stored on the boom ready to hoist, or, in the case of most dinghies, you'll need to rig it and then hoist it. Here's how you prepare a typical mainsail for sailing:

- Remove the mainsail from its bag and unfold it on the deck, dock, or a dry area. Insert the *battens*, the thin strips of fiberglass that support the sail's *roach*.

- Locate the three corners of your sail—the head (top), tack (bottom inside), and clew (bottom outside).

- Attach the head of the sail to the main halyard (most halyards will have some sort of shackle on the end for this purpose).

- Attach the clew to the end of the boom. Typically this is done with a line called the *outhaul*.

- Feed the edge of the mainsail into the groove in the mast. The sail may have individual fittings called *slides* or a continuous *bolt rope*.

- Don't pull the sail all up until you're ready to sail.

- Attach the tack to the fitting (again, the fittings vary—and they could be a hook or piece of line) at the mast end of the boom.

- If the sail is on the boom, remove the sail cover, undo any sail ties and store them all away, and attach the main halyard.

Now you're ready to raise the mainsail.

Hoisting the mainsail.

- Be sure nothing is pulling the sail down—typically this means releasing the mainsheet, the boom vang tension, and checking that reefing lines can run freely.

- Double-check your course. Make sure that you're still pointed into the wind. You'll know if you're not because the sail will start to fill as you raise it. If this happens, stop raising the sail and head back into the wind.

- Hoist the mainsail using the main halyard. Raise the main up by pulling hand over hand. On bigger boats, when it starts to get difficult, wrap the halyard line around a winch and use the winch to gain some mechanical advantage.

- Watch the head of the sail as it rises up the mast—be sure sail slides stay in the mast groove and that no part of the sail gets caught on rigging lines. When the mainsail is fully raised, cleat off the mainsail halyard and *coil* up the line out of the way.

Preparing the Jib for Sailing

Like the mainsail, the jib may be stored off the forestay and require rigging, or it might be set on the forestay on a *furling system*, a storage system in which the sail is wrapped around the forestay and unwound as needed.

On dinghies or more traditional setups, the jib is clipped on to the forestay using *hanks* and is pulled up the mast by a jib halyard. Here is how you prepare the jib for sailing:

- Unroll the jib and identify the three corners. Attach the head of the sail to the jib halyard.

- Starting at the head, clip the hanks to the forestay, being sure to keep them in order. Then attach the tack to the forestay's base. (There will likely be a shackle or line for this purpose.)

- Make sure the two jib sheets are tied to the clew of the sail with a *bowline knot* and run them through the *fairleads* to the *cleats* or winches in the cockpit.

- Pull up the sail with the jib halyard. Let the jib sheets out if needed. When the sail becomes hard to pull up, wrap the halyard around the winch—grind it up until it is taut but not so tight that the material creases and stretches. Cleat off the halyard and coil the line.

- To unfurl a furling jib, wrap the jib sheet around a winch and release the furling line from its brake or clamp. Pull the jib sheet around the winch and let out the furling line gradually so the jib unfurls smoothly but with control.

Setting Sail

Raising the sails is just the first step in sailing. The next step is to work with the wind to get your boat to move. This is done by adjusting the sails.

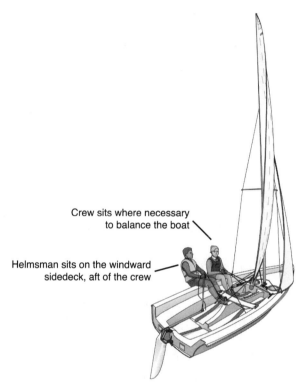

Crew sits where necessary
to balance the boat

Helmsman sits on the windward
sidedeck, aft of the crew

Position of the crew.

Crew positions will vary depending on the conditions, but the helmsmen should sit on the upwind side of the boat and have a clear view past the sails. The crew sits ahead of the skipper and moves from windward to leeward or inward and outward on the boat in an effort to keep it feeling balanced.

So now your boat is pointing into the wind, your sails are raised and shaking in the breeze and, if anything, you're drifting backward a bit. The next step, getting the boat to move, is relatively easy. The key is to maneuver out of *irons*, or what is often called the *no-sail zone*, and angle the boat so the sails catch the wind.

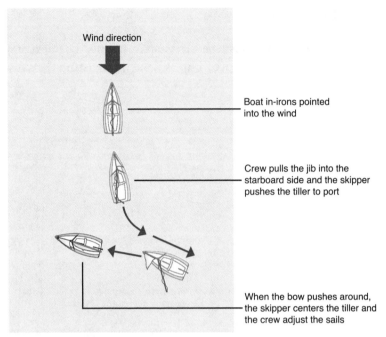

Wind direction

Boat in-irons pointed
into the wind

Crew pulls the jib into the
starboard side and the skipper
pushes the tiller to port

When the bow pushes around,
the skipper centers the tiller and
the crew adjust the sails

Escaping from in-irons.

On a sailing dinghy or small keel boat, catching the wind often can be accomplished by pushing the tiller toward the side of the boat you want the bow to go and pulling the jib sheet to the opposite side so it fills with wind on its reverse side (this is called *backing the jib*). Then when the sail fills, it will pivot the boat into the wind. Once this happens and the wind is 45 degrees or more off the bow, pull in the correct jib sheet, tighten the mainsheet, and let the boat bear off until you're on a beam reach.

A beam reach is a position that lets you easily transition into whatever comes next; the wind comes across the boat's beam, the sails are eased halfway out, the center-board is halfway down, and the skipper and crew are inside the boat. It's a stable point of sail that gives you a chance to get a feel for steering and using the sail controls. But eventually you're going to want to change your course.

SAILOR'S WARNING

Sailing too fast? By easing out the sails when sailing upwind, you will slow your boat and stop *heeling* (tipping). This only works on positions from close hauled through beam reach, though.

Changing course is typically referred to as heading up (bringing the bow closer to the wind) or bearing off and steering away from the wind. Whether you are heading up or bearing off, you need to pay attention to four things: sail trim, centerboard position, crew position, and the course you are making.

Wind direction

Heading up.

When sailing on a beam reach, your sails should be halfway out. If you have a *daggerboard* or centerboard, it should be halfway down and your tiller should be centered.

DEFINITION

A **daggerboard** or centerboard is a retractable keel-like fin under the hull that helps a boat make an upwind course by providing lift and stability.

Wind direction

Head up to a close reach by pushing the tiller away from you, lowering the centerboard to three quarters down, and pulling in the sails. The boat will begin to heel with the force on the sails, so move closer to the windward edge to balance the boat.

Close reach.

Head up further until you are about 45 degrees off the wind. Lower the centerboard fully and sheet both sails tightly—you'll need to sit even further out to balance the boat.

Close hauled.

Bear off to a beam reach by reversing each step. Pull the tiller toward you, ease out the sails, lift up the centerboard, and move closer to the center of the boat.

Beam reach.

Continue to pull the tiller toward you until the wind is coming over the back corner. Raise the centerboard to quarter-down and ease the sails further out.

Broad reach.

Pull the tiller toward you until the wind is coming from directly astern. Raise the centerboard until it's almost all up and ease the main all the way out. You can move the jib to the other side and sail wing-on-wing.

Downwind run.

Trimming Sails

Using the jib sheet or mainsheet to adjust the sails is 90 percent of sail trim. And honestly, there are plenty of sailors who are good with doing only this. But there's more to sail trim than just the sheets. For the main, there's *Cunningham* tension (the Cunningham tightens the sail's luff), *outhaul* tension (the outhaul tightens the mainsail along its *foot*), *traveler* adjustments (the traveler is a track with a moveable car that holds one end of the mainsheet), and *boom vang* tension. (The boom vang pulls the boom down. For the jib, there is the fairlead position and jib halyard tension.

BETTER BOATING

On most sailboats, telltales (small strips of yarn) are found on both sides of the jib's luff. When the sail is trimmed correctly, all of the telltales will stream back, showing that the wind is flowing evenly on both sides of the sail.

If the telltales on one side of the sail are fluttering or hanging limply, you'll need to change your sail trim by adjusting the jib sheet. Knowing what to do is easy—just move the sail in the direction of the limp telltale. If the limp telltales are on the inside of the sail, then pull the jib in tighter. If the limp telltales are on the outside of the sail, then let the jib out.

Each of these adjustments changes the shape of the sail. In some conditions, it's better to have the mainsail very flat, with little *draft* or fullness; tightening the Cunningham, outhaul, and boom vang will do this. Sometimes, if it gets gusty, you'll want the top of the sail twisted away from the bottom to spill off wind; you can do this by pulling the traveler to leeward and easing the sheet to let the boom lift in hard puffs of wind.

NAUTICAL KNOWLEDGE

The pessimist complains about the wind; the optimist expects it to change; the realist adjusts the sails.

—William A. Ward

Use the following table as a guide for sail trim in a variety of weather conditions.

Sail Controls

	Light Wind < 8 kn	Moderate Wind 9–15 kn	Strong or Gusty Wind
Jibsheet Fairlead	Forward	Middle	Aft
Jib Halyard	Light (but sail not saggy)	Moderate	Tight (but no vertical creases in sail)
Main Traveler	To weather	Centered	To Leeward
Boom Vang	Off or Eased	Moderate	Pulled Down Hard
Cunningham	Off	Moderate	Tight (but no creases in sail)
Outhaul	Light	Tight	Tight

Tacking Where You're Going

Eventually every new sailor figures out points of sail and comes up with the same question: "If your destination lies upwind, how do you sail there?"

It works like this: as you sail upwind, trim your sails in tighter to keep them full and to generate lift. But eventually you'll sail too close to the wind, your sails will luff, and your boat will slow down because you've hit the no sail zone. But if you keep turning your bow through the wind, eventually your sails will refill on the other side of the boat. This is called tacking—and by tacking you can reach an upwind destination.

On the new tack, you'll find you're now pointing about a right angle from your old tack, with the wind still at about 45 degrees, but now on the other side of the boat. And by zigzagging upwind, even though the boat can't sail directly into the breeze, you'll reach your destination.

The tricky part with tacking is learning to do it efficiently—there's a lot going on. Not only are you steering through the wind and shifting sails, but the skipper and crew will need to move from one side of the boat to the other.

Wind direction

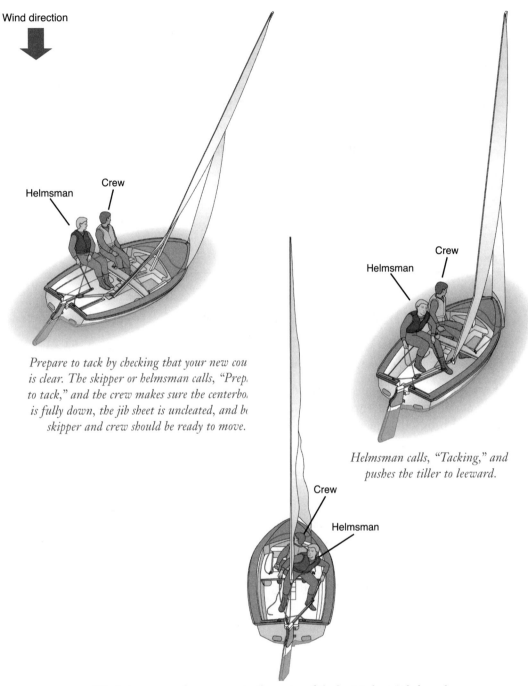

Helmsman   Crew

*Prepare to tack by checking that your new cou...
is clear. The skipper or helmsman calls, "Prep...
to tack," and the crew makes sure the centerbo...
is fully down, the jib sheet is uncleated, and b...
skipper and crew should be ready to move.*

Crew

Helmsman

*Helmsman calls, "Tacking," and
pushes the tiller to leeward.*

Crew

Helmsman

*The helmsman and crew move to the center of the boat to keep it balanced.
When the jib starts to flap (in stronger winds) or back (in lighter winds),
the crew releases the old jib sheet and picks up the new one.*

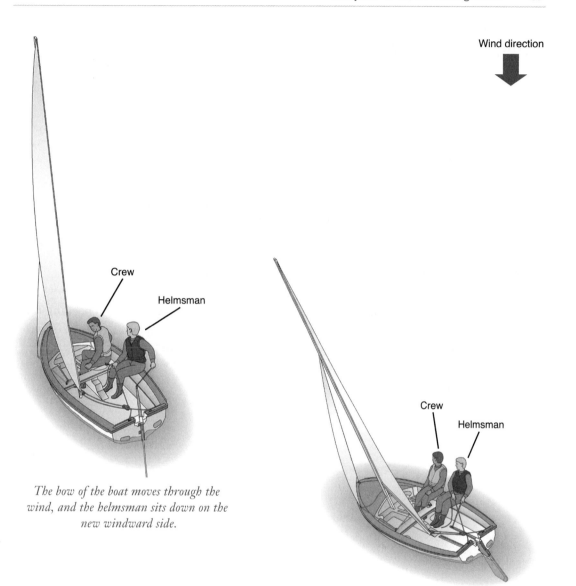

Wind direction

Crew

Helmsman

The bow of the boat moves through the wind, and the helmsman sits down on the new windward side.

Crew

Helmsman

Once the bow of the boat has passed through the wind, the helmsman and crew move into their new positions. The crew pulls in the new jib and the helmsman adjusts the course.

Jibing Onto a New Course

Jibing is the other way to turn your boat, and it's pretty much the opposite of a tack. When you tack, the bow of your boat passes through the wind. During a jibe, the stern passes through the wind.

SAILOR'S WARNING

Which is safer, tacking or jibing?

During a tack, the bow of the boat passes through irons, causing the boat to lose speed and allowing the mainsail to move gently from one side to the other. But when jibing, the boat always has wind in its sails. So the mainsail and boom can slam across to the other side of the boat, increasing the risk of capsize and injury.

But controlling the jibe is easy—just pull in the mainsheet before moving the tiller.

In most ways, a jibe is similar to a tack. You prepare the same way—by checking the course and warning your crew. The main differences are your commands are different, you move the tiller in a different direction, and you must pull the mainsail in before you jibe. Keep in mind that if a jibe seems unsafe, you can always tack.

Wind direction

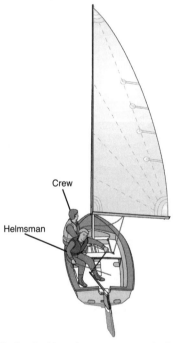

Crew

Helmsman

Prepare to jibe by checking that your course is clear. The helmsman calls, "Prepare to jibe," and the crew makes sure the centerboard is almost fully up, the jib sheet is uncleated, and both skipper and crew are ready to move.

Wind direction

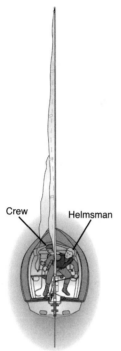

The helmsman and crew move to the center of the boat to keep it balanced. The crew releases the old sheet and picks up the new one. The helmsman eases the mainsail out on the new side.

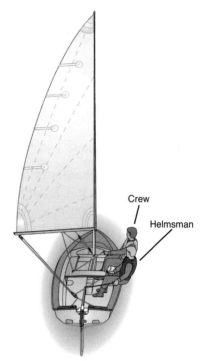

Once the stern of the boat has passed through the wind, the helmsman and crew move into their new positions. The crew pulls in the new jib sheet and the helmsman adjusts the course.

Reefing (or Reducing Sails)

To reef means to reduce or shorten the size of sails. Some longtime boaters will tell you they've never needed to reef. I'm not actually sure how they've managed, but if you own a very stable boat, live in a place with light consistent winds, and never get caught out when they rise—it's possible. For the rest of us, though, any time the wind starts to rise, or you see a squall coming, reefing should be a top priority.

Reefing is a pretty simple concept—basically all you're doing is reducing the amount of sail you have exposed to the wind. On old-time sailboats, reefing was accomplished by dropping some of the sails. But on a modern sloop, which only has two sails, reefing is accomplished by reducing the mainsail size by lowering part of it and gathering up the bottom—a method known as a slab reefing system.

BETTER BOATING

It's always better to reef early and often (and maybe end up with less sail than you need) than to leave too much sail up and potentially be in danger. So don't wait, reef as soon as you think you about it.

When to Reef and How to Reef

There is no hard-and-fast rule about when to reef; it really depends on the boat. A light trailer sailer might start out with a reef if the wind is blowing 12 to 15 knots, while a heavy cruiser might not reef until 20 knots. Keep in mind, when you're sailing downwind, that you may not notice a wind increase. But turning up into the wind can get dicey when you're over canvassed (have too much sail up), so pay attention to changes in the weather.

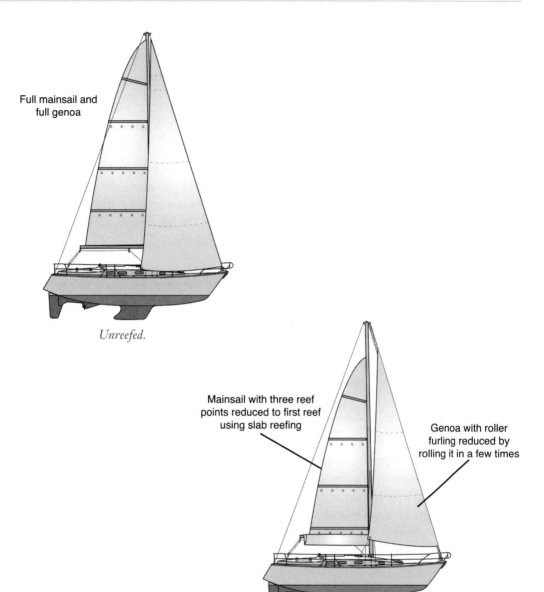

Full mainsail and
full genoa

Unreefed.

Mainsail with three reef
points reduced to first reef
using slab reefing

Genoa with roller
furling reduced by
rolling it in a few times

Reefed.

Both the main and the genoa sails can typically be reefed. Normally (but not always) when you reduce the size of one sail you reduce the size of the other.

The slab reefing system is common on most mainsails and lets you easily reduce sail by one, two, or occasionally three reefs, but it does take practice. Here's what to do:

- Check your course and be aware of any boats or hazards in your area before making course changes.

- Head the boat into the wind and ease the mainsheet until the main sail starts to luff. Be aware, though, that a luffing main can make the boom swing wildly, so keep clear of the motion. Tighten the topping lift (the line that supports the end of the boom) and loosen the boom vang (the line that holds down the boom).

- Slowly lower the main halyard, while simultaneously pulling in the reefing control line. This will pull the bottom of the mainsail down to the boom and make the triangle of sail much smaller. On some sails, you simply pull down the front of the sail when the halyard is lowered and only a leech reef line is pulled in.

- When the sail is reduced to the reef points (some sails have one, while others have two or three), secure the new tack (usually there is a hook) and then secure the reefing line and retighten the halyard, go back on course, and trim the sail. Remember to ease the topping lift and trim the boom vang if needed.

Reducing a *roller furling jib* (a sail that wraps around the wire at the front of the boat) or genoa is pretty much the same as rolling it in when you're done using it. Head into the wind and ease the sheet, pull in on the roller furling line until the sail is the size you want, go back on course, and adjust the sheet trim. If you are sailing away from the wind, ease the jib sheet a large amount until the sail starts fluttering and then pull in the roller furling line.

Increasing Sail

Shaking out, or letting out a reef, when the wind has dropped is a matter of reversing the basic reefing steps:

- Turn the boat into the wind and ease the mainsheet until the sail luffs. Lower the main halyard by 6 inches.

- Unhook the tack. Uncleat the reefing line and pull the halyard to raise the mainsail back up.

- When the sail is back up, secure the halyard.

- If you want to ease out the genoa as well, ease the sheet some and gradually release the roller furling line until the sail is back out.

- Go back on course and adjust sail trim.

Heaving To

Heaving to is often thought of as an emergency procedure for boats caught out in a storm. The tactic, which allows you to slow your boat by putting the sails and rudder in opposition to each other, reduces a boat's rough motion and reduces the stress on the sailing gear and the crew.

While most new sailors rightly assume that they are unlikely to be in an offshore storm where heaving to is useful, keep in mind heaving to has other purposes which makes it well worth learning. Boats that are sailing don't have brakes and don't really have the ability to stop, unless you heave to. For example, if you arrive at a river bar before slack water, or if you want to enjoy your lunch without having to constantly steer and tweak the sails, heaving to is a simple option.

Heaving to is a little different on every boat and can take a bit of practice. The goal is to modify the following steps until you balance your boat:

- Slow your boat down by heading up until both sails are luffing.

- Tack the boat without releasing the jib.

- The main should be full on one side and the jib should be backwinded on the other.

- Move the tiller so you are attempting to steer upwind. Make tiller adjustments until your boat balances (doesn't tack or bear off), with the bow pointed slightly into the waves.

- Lash the tiller in place.

So now your boat is steering to windward. As the boat rounds up, the main loses power, while at the same time the backwinded jib is pushing your boat backward. So you're steering a meandering course to windward but your boat is actually being pushed downwind and drifting sideways. In bad weather this sideways motion disturbs the water and creates an upwind slick that reduces the roughness of waves.

Recovering from a Capsize

If you sail a dinghy, at some point you're going to capsize. Either you'll move too slowly or a gust of wind will catch you. Capsizes are so common in dinghy sailing that recovering from them is one of the first skills taught when you take a dinghy sailing class. Some dinghies—high-powered racing dinghies or very small tippy ones—are more likely to capsize, while larger general-purpose dinghies are less likely to.

The goal with a capsize is to right it as quickly as possible without giving the boat time to turn completely upside down. The way you do this is to counteract the forces on the sail by adding your weight to the daggerboard or centerboard.

The crew makes sure the centerboard is all the way down. The helmsmen secures the rudder.

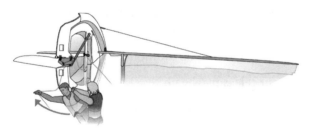

The heaviest person swims around the stern of the boat to the centerboard.

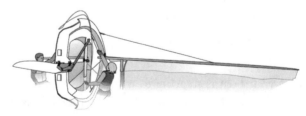

The light person tosses the top jib sheet to the person at the centerboard to help them with climbing up.

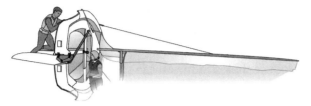

The person on the centerboard climbs up. Their weight will pull the boat upright, so they should be ready to climb into the boat as it comes up.

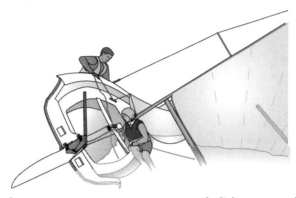

As the boat comes up, you can attempt to scoop the lighter person aboard while the person on the centerboard climbs in. You should move slowly and carefully because the boat will be filled with water and be easy to recapsize.

Once aboard, use a bailer or the self-bailing drains to empty the water out. If the boat has turned over completely, the procedure is roughly the same—except both crew will be needed on the centerboard to lever the boat upright.

The Least You Need to Know

- Points of sail and the corresponding sail trim are guidelines, not a precise science. Every boat is a little different.
- Tacking is the act of turning your bow through the wind and adjusting your crew position and sails to the new course.

- Jibing is the opposite of tacking; your stern passes through the wind but carries more risks because your sails stay filled with wind and the boom can slam across the boat if not controlled.

- Reefing the sails allows you to reduce their size so you can sail more safely in stronger winds.

- Heaving to is a basic skill that allows you to stop the boat by putting the sails and tiller in opposition to each other.

- Capsizing a dingy is a common occurrence, and knowing how to recover is important.

Heading Out

In This Chapter

- Following a predeparture checklist
- Motoring away from the dock
- Understanding prop walk and pivot points
- Returning to the dock
- Launching your boat from a ramp (and returning)

It's a lovely day: the sky is blue, the sun is warm, the sea beckons, and you want to fling off the dock lines and head out and test your new skills. Launching a boat for the first time can be exciting—and a bit nerve wracking.

I'll never forget one of the first times my husband and I left the dock. In our excitement we skipped our predeparture checklist and never noticed there was a strong breeze blowing on our beam. Instead, we pulled out into the channel and were immediately swept sideways. We wanted to save ourselves by hooking another boat with the boat hook. Unfortunately this important piece of safety equipment was still stashed down below and we lost valuable moments searching for it.

Luckily our lesson came without any cost—but what we learned is to always go through our checklist, always make a plan before untying any lines, and to practice. Learning to leave the dock/launch ramp/mooring without drama will make your entire sailing experience more enjoyable.

Developing a Predeparture Checklist You'll Use

Every time you set off on your boat you need to make sure you and the boat are ready to go. This is one of those "for the want of a horseshoe nail" things, because all too often it's one insignificant-seeming detail that leads to a cascading series of problems. In our case, heading out into a strong wind led to the realization that we hadn't put out our safety equipment, and if I hadn't found the boat hook when I did (which was disassembled and stored away) we would have hit a rock wall.

Obviously checking off items on a list isn't going to head off every potential problem, but ensuring you have the necessary safety equipment, that your boat's mechanical systems are functioning, and that you are properly prepared are important steps toward being safe on the water. And if you own your own boat, developing a unique list that takes into account *your* boat's specific requirements is an important first step in ownership.

Many people choose to post their predeparture checklist in an obvious location such as near the engine's ignition switch or on the chart table. Here's an example of a predeparture checklist you might post:

Example Predeparture Checklist

Engine:

- Open any sea cocks (an underwater valve that lets in water) that have been closed.
- Check fuel levels ($\frac{1}{3}$ to go out, $\frac{1}{3}$ to come back, $\frac{1}{3}$ spare).

Navigation:

- Obtain weather forecast and discuss it with crew.
- Check tides and currents.
- File a float plan with family or friends.
- Plan your course on navigational charts and check for hazards.

DEFINITION

A *float plan* isn't an official document, it simply means telling someone on shore about your planned route and when to expect you back. Then if something happens and you don't show up as expected, the person with your float plan can pass the information on to the Coast Guard—who will then start to look out for you. Include your name, mobile phone number, and the names of who is aboard with you; where you launched from; and where you will be boating, any intended stops, and when you will be back. Give a detailed description of your boat that includes the color, name, year, make and model, registration numbers, and anything else distinctive (sail cover color, dinghy on deck, sail numbers). *And don't forget to check in once you get back to shore!*

Safety:

- Check that you have proper-fitting PFDs (personal flotation devices) for all aboard.

- Locate and check condition of safety equipment: distress signals, fire extinguisher, whistle, bilge pump, rigging knife, etc.

- Make sure on-deck safety equipment is in place: man overboard equipment, boat hook, etc.

- Secure things down below: latch lockers, store away gear.

Electronics:

- Test navigation lights, compass light, VHF radio, etc.

Sails:

- Get the jib hanked on, sheets run, and jib halyard connected and ready to hoist.

- Be sure the main halyard is connected and ready to hoist.

Paperwork:

- Locate vessel paperwork: state registration, insurance, and license.

Leaving the Dock

Unless you have a small sailboat without a motor, most sailboats use the engine when they leave the dock, especially in modern marinas which are often both labyrinthine and jam-packed. So after going through your predeparture checklist and readying the sails, it's time to fire up the engine, make sure it's running smoothly, and plan your departure from the dock.

Leaving a dock (or coming into one) can be a display of good boating skills or an embarrassing exhibit that can cause boat damage or injury. The key is in preparation and in taking it slow. It takes longer to stop your boat than a car, so you need to move slowly—with just enough throttle to provide forward momentum and steerage in the direction you need to go. One popular saying is, "If you're not getting bored, you're going too fast."

Before you untie any dock lines, you need to know four things:

- Where is the wind (or current) coming from and where is it going to push your bow?
- What sort of traffic is around, and where are they going?
- What is your plan of action, step by step?
- What is the role of each person on board? And do they know their jobs?

A Few Notes About Steering

New boaters are often caught off guard when they drive a boat because boats don't act at all like cars do. One issue is *prop walk*. An inboard engine propeller usually turns clockwise (if you looked at it from the back) and is said to be "right-handed." This means when the engine is in forward gear, even if the rudder is straight, the stern will push slightly to starboard; in reverse gear the action is much stronger, and the stern moves noticeably to port.

Another issue is boats don't turn the way cars do—they pivot. And the pivot point moves. When a boat is moving forward, the pivot point is often one third back from the bow, near the mast. When it's in reverse, the pivot point is one third forward of the stern.

The reason I'm telling you about prop walk and pivot points is some maneuvers are going to be easier than others. For example, it's easier to back away from a dock that's on your starboard side because the prop walks the stern to port. But if you power forward, your stern will swing toward the dock and can bump—unless you push the stern off first.

Working With Wind and Current

In typical conditions, boats are tied up with a bow line, stern line, bow spring, and stern spring. In some conditions breast ropes are added. Lines are not just for tying up, though—you can use them to position your boat for a safe departure.

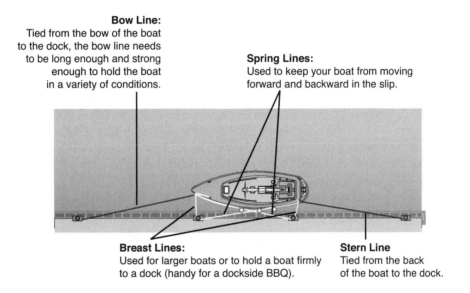

Bow Line:
Tied from the bow of the boat to the dock, the bow line needs to be long enough and strong enough to hold the boat in a variety of conditions.

Spring Lines:
Used to keep your boat from moving forward and backward in the slip.

Breast Lines:
Used for larger boats or to hold a boat firmly to a dock (handy for a dockside BBQ).

Stern Line
Tied from the back of the boat to the dock.

When the wind or current is pushing your boat from ahead or away from the dock, leaving is straightforward:

- Have one crew cast off your stern lines and toss them in the cockpit. (They can coil them later.)

- Then have your other crew cast off your bow lines while you give a short burst in forward gear. Tell your crew to come aboard as you move slowly out of your slip.

- If you need to make a turn into a channel, add power then wait until you are nearing two thirds of the way out of your slip and turn.

- Be sure to bring in your lines and fenders (the bumpers that protect your boat at a dock) and store them away.

If the wind or current is pushing your boat from astern toward the dock, the procedure changes a bit:

- Cast off all lines except the stern spring line. This line will keep you from moving forward and allow the stern to pivot away from the dock (slide a fender forward to cushion the bow).

- Turn the tiller to push the stern away from the dock.

- Shift into forward gear. The stern should swing away from the dock. Shift into reverse, cast off the spring line, and back further from the dock.

- When safely clear, shift into forward and idle away from the dock.

Motoring Back to the Dock

Returning to the dock is pretty much just the reverse of leaving. Before entering the marina, have your crew put the fenders back out and then have them get all the dock lines out and readied. Assign one crew to the bow with a fender (for a possible collision with another docked boat). Also ask them to help you spot the slip and give direction if you require.

SAILOR'S WARNING

Never use your legs, feet, or arms to fend off a collision. Boats, unlike cars, do not have brakes to help them stop, and even a small boat carries a lot of momentum. Your body is way too tender to be a fender.

At this stage, you and your crew should have analyzed conditions and developed a plan. Basically, you need everyone else to know their jobs so you can concentrate on steering. If you have a choice, it's easiest to come into a dock with your bow into the wind or current, letting it slow you as you approach.

If you're headed to a port side, tie up approach at about a 25-degree angle with a fender on the bow, slow the engine, touch the bow gently to the dock, and give it a little reverse engine (straight rudder or turned to starboard); the prop wash should push your stern to the dock. Have your crew step (never leap) onto the dock and secure lines.

If you're coming in on a starboard dock, use a narrower approach to avoid needing to reverse. Touch the fendered starboard bow to the dock gently and turn the rudder to port to bring in your stern.

Often there will be someone on the dock who will offer to catch your dock lines. Let them help, but always double-check the cleats yourself. You'll want to adjust your lines anyway, making sure the boat is sitting just right in her slip.

BETTER BOATING

Practice docking on open water—find a buoy or float to use as a landmark and practice "docking" in a variety of conditions: backing in, into the wind, with the wind on your beam, etc.

Docking at a Mooring

Mooring buoys are typically floating round balls attached to some sort of underwater heavy base. Mooring fields can contain numerous buoys (typically numbered) that are often sized for different types of boats.

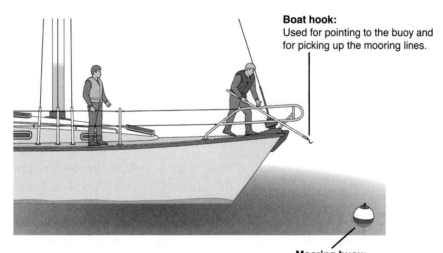

Boat hook:
Used for pointing to the buoy and for picking up the mooring lines.

Mooring buoy:
Look for a short line in the water or a top ring to attach your lines to.

Mooring fields can look intimidating at first glance, but basic docking skills still apply; have a plan and approach slowly. The most common mistake while picking up a mooring is approaching too fast. You can't go too slow (if you do you just speed up), but you can overshoot the mooring, which can cause you to get caught up in it. Here's how you dock at a mooring:

- Slowly approach the buoy from downwind and/or down current. If the wind and current are going in different directions, decide which one is strongest.

- Once the mooring ball is at your bow, slow down or gently reverse.

- Have your crew reach for the pickup line with your boat hook. Some moorings require you to pass your own dock line through the eye of the mooring and back to your vessel. You may want to use your own line if the mooring pennants are worn or encrusted with marine growth.

To leave your mooring, make note of the wind and current, turn on your engine, then simply untie yourself from the mooring and motor away.

BETTER BOATING

When possible, cruise by your mooring to check it out before making an attempt to pick it up. Note the type and condition of the mooring ball and how the wind and current will affect your approach.

Setting Off from a Launching Ramp

Launching dinghies or small keelboats from a boat ramp using a trailer can take a bit of practice to get right—but can open up a larger cruising ground.

Driving or pushing a trailer backward down a steep, potentially slippery ramp doesn't sound easy, and without practice, it's probably even harder. A good idea might be to have a pro teach you a few techniques before you even try. Once you're comfortable enough to try launching on your own, choose a quiet ramp that's not too steep and that has a dock beside it. If you are launching a dinghy from a hand trailer, it's still handy to have a dock—or at least a sandy beach that you can launch from.

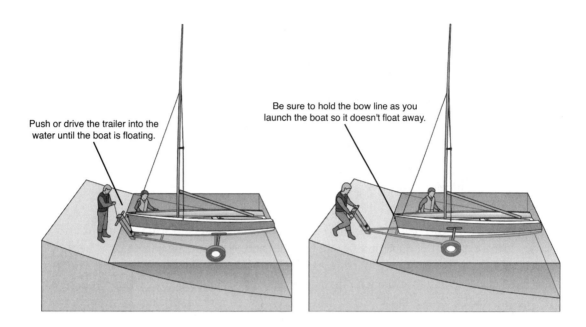

Here are a few hints and techniques to get you off the street and into the water:

- Prepare your boat for launching away from the ramp. Raise mast, put on the sails, connect the fuel tank, and check safety equipment.

- Raise the outboard so that it will not hit bottom during launching.

- Make sure that the winch is ready and the tie downs are removed.

- Put the drain plug in securely.

- Disconnect the trailer lights.

- Attach bow and stern lines so that your boat cannot drift away after launching and it can be easily secured to the dock.

- Inspect the launch ramp for hazards including potholes, a steep drop-off, or slippery patches.

- Maneuver the boat slowly to the ramp, keeping in mind that your boat is just resting on the trailer and attached only at the bow.

- Keep the rear wheels of the tow vehicle out of the water so the exhaust pipes stay dry.

- Set the parking brake.

- Lower the motor (if you have one) and start it.

- Release the winch and disconnect the winch line from the bow. The boat should launch with a light shove; make sure someone is holding the bow line.

- Return the towing vehicle and trailer to the parking lot and finish any final details at the dock or at the beach.

Many small trailer-launched sailboats don't have engines, and while it's a little trickier to learn to sail off a dock or a beach, the skills are the same. If your boat is being blown sideways against the dock, it can be almost impossible to get started. You'll need to maneuver into the wind to raise the sails—or paddle away from the dock to get started.

Returning to the Launching Ramp

Getting your boat back out of the water is basically launching in reverse.

 SAILOR'S WARNING

Keep in mind that conditions change during the day so make note of changes in wind direction and/or speed, a change in current and/or tide height, and increases in boating traffic.

- Remove the sails and unpack the boat at the dock.

- Maneuver the boat to your submerged trailer, and raise the motor.

- Winch the boat onto the trailer.

- Drive the trailer with the boat aboard carefully out of the water and up the ramp for cleanup, reloading, and an equipment safety check.

- Pull the drain plug.

- Secure the boat for street travel.

The Least You Need to Know

- A predeparture checklist should include all the safety and mechanical checks you need to make before leaving the dock.
- The key to leaving the dock safely is having a plan and taking it slow.
- Driving a boat is very different than driving a car, as a boat pivots, it doesn't turn, it experiences prop walk (which pushes the stern sideways), and it doesn't have brakes, so it can be hard to stop.
- Picking up a mooring is easiest when you go slowly and aim into the current or wind.
- Using a boat launch is a good way to access a wider area in a small boat—but you'll need to learn how to launch your boat and return it to the boat ramp.

Anchoring Your Boat

In This Chapter

- Choosing an anchor
- Planning where to anchor
- Staying put
- Retrieving your anchor

Not long ago I helped a neighbor untie his docklines so he could head out for a sail. I was a bit surprised when I looked his boat over and realized he had no anchor in his bow roller (the storage place for the anchor). I asked if the anchor was stored somewhere else and he'd forgotten to put it in place. He said no, he'd gotten rid of the anchor because for day sails it was in the way and he didn't think he needed it.

Later that day he returned—towed in by a towing company. It turned out his engine had stopped and there wasn't enough wind for him to sail back against the current. He said he was immediately going to go buy a new anchor, because if he had had one he could have anchored and waited for the wind to come up. Or perhaps he could have even fixed his engine and avoided a big towing bill.

If you have a small boat and only sail in fair weather, you might feel that you can do without safety equipment like anchors or tow lines, and that you don't have to worry about developing more advanced skills, such as squall management and reducing sail. But boating can be unpredictable, and being prepared for anything is a big part of staying safe.

How to Choose an Anchorage

There are many reasons to anchor; staying somewhere for the afternoon or overnight is the most common. But boats will also anchor to sit out bad weather, to wait for the tide to turn, to make a repair, or to manage an emergency.

Where you anchor can vary as dramatically as why you anchor. But the ideal anchorage should be protected from the prevailing wind and waves. The preferred bottom (sea floor) can be made up of mud, sand, or clay, but should be free of rock, coral, or weed. Regional cruising guides will often highlight good anchorages, but even nautical charts can offer many clues, indicating the composition of the bottom, water depths, and hazards.

NAUTICAL KNOWLEDGE

It's important to note that the anchorage marks on most nautical charts are intended for large ships and that those locations may not be suitable for smaller boats.

When you are picking a spot to anchor, you need to be aware of a number of factors:

- How deep is the water? How much will the depth change while you're there? Check the tide table to know for sure. (See Chapter 4 for more information on calculating tides.)

- What is the bottom like? Most anchors can dig into firm mud and sand but have trouble holding in rock, weeds, or coral. Check the nautical chart and look for the symbol that indicates what's down there (more on reading charts in Chapter 9).

- Are there hazards such as submerged rocks, sunken wrecks, underwater cables, or overhead power lines that are too low for your mast to safely pass under?

- Which way is the wind blowing? Is it forecast to change? Will you have sufficient *swing room* if it does change?

- Where are other boats anchored in relation to your boat? Try to anchor near boats of a similar size and type and with a similar amount of *scope* to help you swing in a similar manner.

DEFINITION

Swing room describes the amount of space your boat needs at anchor. The place you drop your anchor is the center of the area you may swing through and around. The amount of **scope** (the length of chain or rope) you put down will determine how far you'll reach out from that center point. And the total swing room is the potential circle you can swing around the anchor.

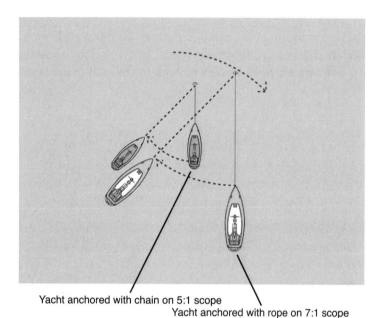

Yacht anchored with chain on 5:1 scope

Yacht anchored with rope on 7:1 scope

Yachts lie clear of each other until the wind shifts, when they are in danger of colliding. Avoid anchoring close to other yachts, especially if they are of a different type or have a different cable or scope from yours.

When anchoring near other boats, you need to calculate your swing area compared to theirs. It you have less scope or a different sort and length of rode (or anchor line—chain versus rope, for example), or if you are a different size and type of boat you'll swing differently.

Choosing an Anchor and Setting It Right

Not all anchors are created equal. The most obvious differences are seen in their size, shape, and weight. But different anchors also have various pros and cons: some store more easily, while others are more affordable; some set better in mud or weed, while others dig into sand better; some will hold tight in a blow, but can trip (break free) in a big wind shift.

If you head into a marine store, you'll see many different anchor choices. Basically, though, they boil down to a few main types. You'll also see a variety of poorly made knock-offs, but with anchors it's best to stick to the well-made brand names. Here are six:

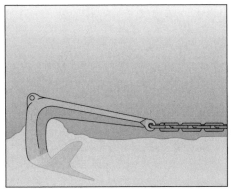

Bruce anchor.

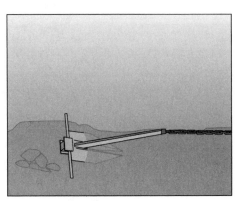

Danforth anchor.

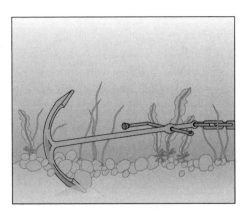

Fisherman's anchor.

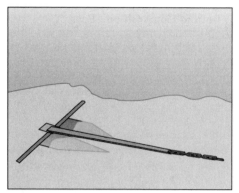

Fortress anchor.

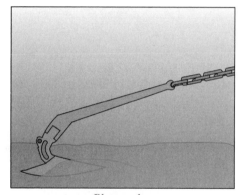

Plow anchor.

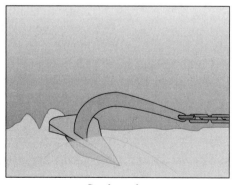

Spade anchor.

Different Anchors for Different Conditions

Anchor Type	Bottom Composition	Pros	Cons
Danforth or Fortress	Clay, sand, and mud	Good weight-to-strength ratio. Easy to store because it lies flat. Very popular.	Can come undone in a large shift in the direction of pull from the boat, such as in tide change or wind change. The anchor will not set on a hard, rocky, or weedy bottom when the flukes can't bury.
Plow or CQR	Sand, thick mud or clay, pebbles, and coral	Resists pulling out when the direction of pull changes. Very robust.	Bulkier to store than a Danforth. Has a hinge that can get blocked, which can cause it to not set properly or to pull out. In large or abrupt direction changes the anchor can roll and pull out.
Delta or Bruce	Similar to a Plow/CQR but better in softer mud.	In some conditions has stronger holding power than the Plow/CQR. Not having the hinge makes it easier to handle. Less expensive than a plow.	Heavier and bulkier than Danforth anchors.
Grapnel, Fortress	Coral, stone, and heavy vegetation	Useful in coral or where the flukes can grip something. Often selected when an anchor is a safety requirement but not needed. Lightweight and inexpensive.	Not very useful in most conditions.

Anchor Type	Bottom Composition	Pros	Cons
Rocna, Manson Supreme, Wasi, Bügel, Sarca Spade	All	Called "next generation" anchors because they are useful in all situations and have superior holding/resetting characteristics.	More expensive. Some early versions had quality issues.
Fisherman, Mushroom	Varied		Specialty anchors that are not typically suited to sailboats.

Once you decide on the type of anchor you want, use the manufacturer's guidelines to select the correct size of anchor and the best type and amount of rode to use.

Anchoring and Staying Put—Until You're Ready to Go

The first few times we anchored, I had trouble believing that a small metal object had any hope of holding my boat in place. But then we sat out a fairly strong blow and I became convinced. Traditionally anchors worked by using their weight to keep a boat from drifting. More modern anchors work a bit differently—they bury themselves in the bottom to develop the holding power that stops a boat from moving.

Anchoring Words

Just like every other aspect of sailing, anchoring also has its own distinct set of words to describe everything from the rope that connects the anchor to the boat to what we are doing when we anchor. Here are a few of them:

- *Ground tackle:* The anchors, chain, rope, and fittings used in anchoring a boat
- *Rode:* The chain, rope, or combination that attaches your boat to the anchor
- *Bitter end:* The end of the rode attached to your boat
- *Scope:* The ratio of the length of rode to the water depth

- *Weigh anchor:* Lifting the anchor from the sea floor; similar to "anchors aweigh" (not "anchors away")

- *Drag:* When the anchor has broken off the bottom and your boat is unintentionally underway

- *Set:* Dropping and positioning your anchor so that it digs in and holds

- *Chocks and bow roller:* A storage place for the anchor on the bow

- *Windlass:* A mechanical device (can be electric or manual) that helps winch up a heavy anchor

Setting and Retrieving Your Anchor

Like most aspects of boating, safe anchoring begins before you leave the dock. You need to be sure your anchor is set up properly, with the bitter end of the rode securely attached to the boat and the other end attached to an anchor that's either up on the bow or in some other accessible area.

Steps to anchoring your boat:

- Select an area to anchor that has plenty of room and has adequate water depth. Ideally, it should be a well-protected area with a sandy or muddy bottom and be free of hazards and outside of navigable waterways such as a channel.

- Measure the depth of the water using your depth sounder and double-check your nautical chart for water depth and add to this number the distance from the level of your depth sounder (most are a foot or two underwater) to the top of your bow. (See Chapter 10 for a discussion of depth sounders.) Take into account any amount the tide will rise from this initial number. So, if you are in 12 feet of water and the distance from the depth sounder to your deck is 4 feet and you have arrived at mid tide and expect the tide to rise 3 feet more, this number will be 12 + 4 + 3, or 19 feet.

- Determine the amount of scope you want to let out using a minimum ratio of 3:1 for all-chain rode (4:1 is better), and you should aim for up to 7:1 for rope. In other words, you set your scope at a minimum of three times the water depth, also factoring in tide and deck height (19 feet for our example). So if you use a 7:1 ratio, the scope would be 133 feet (7 × 19). (When you have the room, always err on the side of more scope.)

- Motor slowly into the wind or current to a position upwind or up-current of the spot you chose. If you tried to drop your anchor right where you wanted to end up, you would find yourself in the wrong place. This takes practice—but if you are letting out 133 feet of rode, motoring 60 to 80 feet past your spot should get you back to it.

- When you are in position, stop the boat and slowly lower the anchor over the bow until it reaches the bottom. Double-check that the bitter end is securely attached to the boat.

- Let the anchor rode run out gradually as you back the boat slowly downwind or down-current until you have let out the desired scope. If you let the anchor rode out all at once, it would simply pile up on the bottom, potentially tangling up and not setting.

- Secure the line around a bow cleat, and slowly increase the motor speed in reverse—this will dig your anchor in to set it.

- Take visual sightings of onshore objects or buoys in the water to help you know where your boat is positioned. When the rode is taut and your boat is motionless, slow the engine down and put it in neutral. (You'll spring forward when this happens—but don't worry.)

- Recheck your sightings frequently or set a GPS anchor alarm to make sure the anchor is not dragging.

- Don't leave the boat until it's had a chance to settle in for a while. Occasionally you'll get a false set—where the anchor hooks on a rock or reef, then slips off. If we know bad weather is coming or conditions allow, we'll dive on our anchor and look at the set in person.

To raise your anchor (in case of dragging or because you're ready to go), start your motor and slowly approach the anchor site while your crew pulls on the anchor. When the bow is directly above the anchor, pulling upward on the anchor rode should break it free. If not, slowly motor forward or turn in a circle with the anchor line held (or cleated) tight. When the anchor does break free, bring it aboard and secure it before getting underway.

Helping Hand Signals

Engine noise and distance between crew means anchoring communication often ends up as yelling—which is never a good thing on a boat. Using hand signals has saved more than a few sailing relationships. There are loads of variations on hand signals, but on my boat we like these:

- "Go that way: Point where you want the boat to go. Always point where you want the boat to go and not at a hazard.

- "Slow down": With your palm facing down and arm out to the side, slowly lower your hand.

- "Speed up": With your palm facing up, lift your hand.

- "Go ahead": Pat your head to indicate you want the driver to put the engine in forward gear.

- "Reverse": Pat your backside to indicate reverse.

- "Neutral": Indicate you want the boat in neutral with a raised fist.

The Least You Need to Know

- An anchor is an essential piece of safety equipment, so choose one that suits your boat and the type of conditions you'll need it in.

- A good anchorage should be protected from the wind and waves, have the right depth of water for your boat, and have a sea bottom that provides good holding.

- Anchoring and ending up exactly where you want can take a great deal of practice.

- Learning hand signals will make communication while anchoring easier and more clear.

Sailing Safely

In This Chapter

- Learning to stay out of trouble
- Following the safety requirements for your boat
- Avoiding common mishaps
- Knowing what to do if you get in trouble
- Coping in adverse conditions
- Getting a tow

Calling the Coast Guard for help was one of those things we never expected to do. But when we took our heavily renovated boat out for her initial *shakedown voyage*—we found ourselves sinking. After searching unsuccessfully for the leak, and not being able to get ahead of the water, we called a *Pan Pan*. While we waited for the Coast Guard, we located a leaking engine fitting and made the repair. By the time help arrived, we only needed a salvage pump to clear the water.

Listen in to the U.S. Coast Guard on VHF Channel 16 on any afternoon and it will soon become apparent that we are not alone; boaters get into plenty of trouble. From groundings to capsizes, in 2010 the U.S. Coast Guard recorded 4,604 recreational boating mishaps and accidents.

What surprised me is, according to U.S. Coast Guard stats, it's just not inclement weather or dangerous waters that do us in. Instead, a boat is most likely to get into trouble on a Saturday afternoon in July when the sun is shining and the weather is calm. Those are the days when recreational boaters are out in the greatest numbers, and it turns out those benign summer conditions might just lull us into a sense of complacency.

Take a Safe Boating Class

It may seem obvious, but a safe and fun boating trip begins well before the dock lines are untied. In the United States, less than 10 percent of serious boating incidents happen to boaters who have had some sort of safety training. So being prepared can come with a big payback.

And keep in mind that taking a class might not be optional—over half of the 50 U.S. states now make boating safety education mandatory, and The Pleasure Craft Operator Card is required for all recreational boaters in Canada.

These basic courses don't teach sailing skills. (They focus on safety, navigation, rules of the road, fueling, docking, and more.) But they can prepare you for a safe day on the water, and they also have another role: they help identify areas of your boat and boating that you're not familiar with and hopefully promote lifelong learning on topics like engine maintenance, coastal navigation, and first aid.

Here are some websites to help you find a safe boating class:

- Boat U.S. Foundation: boatus.com/foundation
- National Association of State Boating Law Administrators: nasbla.org
- National Safe Boating Council: safeboatingcouncil.org
- United States Power Squadrons: usps.org
- U.S. Coast Guard Auxiliary: cgaux.org

Legally Required (and Good to Have) Safety Equipment

Once you know what you're doing, the next step is to make sure your boat is prepared. Should the Coast Guard stop you and board your boat while you're underway, they can terminate your trip or give you a citation if they discover you are missing some of the safety requirements or equipment.

The following table includes is the minimum safety gear for recreational boats:

U.S. Coast Guard Minimum Requirements for Recreational Boats

Equipment	Boats less than 16ft/4.9m	16 to less than 26 ft/4.9–7.9m	26 to less than 40 ft/7.9–12.2m	40 to not more than 65 ft/12.2–19.8m
State Registration or Federal Documentation	All boats need to be either state registered or federally documented. If you're state registered, make sure the paperwork is on the boat when it's in use. You'll also need your registration number clearly marked on your hull. If the boat is documented, the name and hailing port must be on the stern and the official number needs to be inside.			
Personal Flotation Devices (PFDs) Note that children under 13 need to wear an approved PFD whenever a recreational boat is underway, unless they are below decks or in a closed cabin.	One approved Type I, II, III, or V PFD for each person on board.	One approved Type I, II, or III PFD for each person on board; and one throwable Type IV device.		
Sound-Producing Device	All boats less than 65.6 ft. (20 m) in length must carry some sort of sound-producing device such as an air horn or whistle. (Yelling isn't acceptable.)			
Visual Distress Signals	Must carry an electric distress light or three day/night flares if out between sunset and sunrise.	Carry one orange distress flag and one electric distress light, or three handheld or floating orange smoke signals and one electric distress light, or three combination (day/night) red flares: handheld, meteor, or parachute type.		

continues

U.S. Coast Guard Minimum Requirements for Recreational Boats (continued)

Equipment	Boats less than 16ft/4.9m	16 to less than 26 ft/4.9–7.9m	26 to less than 40 ft/7.9–12.2m	40 to not more than 65 ft/12.2–19.8m
Fire Extinguisher (Must be Coast Guard–approved)	One B-I type fire extinguisher if your boat has an inboard engine, compartments where combustible materials are stored, closed living spaces, or permanently installed fuel tanks.		Two B-I type *or* one B-II type portable fire extinguishers.	Three B-I type *or* one B-I type *plus* one B-II type portable fire extinguishers.
Oil Pollution and Garbage Placard	Must be displayed in a conspicuous location aboard.			
Inboard Engine Ventilation **Gasoline Powered**	If your boat has a gasoline engine and was built after July 31, 1980, you'll need an exhaust blower. If built before this time it can have natural ventilation provided by two ducts.			
Navigational Lights	Must be displayed from sunset to sunrise.			
Backfire Flame Arrestor	One approved device on each carburetor of any inboard gasoline engine installed after April 25, 1940.			
Marine Sanitation Device	If there is a toilet aboard, it must be a type I, II, or III.			

Keep in mind different states may have additional requirements, so check your local regulations.

Voluntary Safety Checks

Once you've made sure that you have all your safety equipment and that it's up to date and in good working order, you can get a decal to prove it. Safety checks provided by the U.S. Coast Guard Auxiliary are educational and informational—meaning if you're missing something vital, you get a written report of the deficiency, not a citation.

The checks do frequently turn up problems—finding safety gear that's missing, not in good working order, or that's not readily accessible. But if you pass the check, you're given a decal that informs authorities (and your insurance company) that your boat is in full compliance with all federal and state boating laws. Keep in mind you'll need a new check (and decal) each calendar year.

To find an examiner in your region, contact the U.S. Coast Guard Auxiliary: cgaux.org/vsc.

> **SAILOR'S WARNING**
>
> Safety equipment must be maintained in good condition and be accessible at all times. As the captain of your boat, it's your responsibility to ensure that you and your passengers know:
>
> - Where it is stowed
> - How to use it
> - When to use it

Additional Safety Equipment

Just because something isn't required does not mean it's not a good idea. Check this list for additional safety equipment:

- Alternative Propulsion: On a small sailboat, having a spare outboard, oars, or paddles to get the boat to safety is essential. Sails are great but sometimes the wind just doesn't do what you want it to.

- Bailer or Bilge Pump: Ever heard the saying, keep the boat in the water and the water out of the boat? Well, you'll need some method to get water out. Bailers, buckets, and bilge pumps should be on every boat.

- First Aid Kit: In the event of injury it can take time to get help, so having a first aid kit that meets your minimum onboard needs is essential. Consider including sunscreen and seasickness medication along with the standard items.

- Flashlight: Always useful at night, it's also handy to have a flashlight for checking bilges or repairing engines.

- Fresh Water: Water is essential all the time, but when boating in the sun and salt, it's easy to become dehydrated. Make sure that your water is fresh and clean and kept in a suitable reusable container.

- Knife: Knives are so handy on sailboats there are specialized sailing and rigging knives available from marine stores. Most fold into some sort of sheath and lack a sharp tip to avoid accidents.

- Magnetic Compass: GPS's have replaced compasses in many areas of navigation but having a compass is still an important part of coastal navigation.

- Radar Reflector: Radar reflectors help other boats "see" your boat. Sailboats are often made from GRP (Glass Reinforced Plastic) and don't show up on the radar screens of other vessels. Having a radar reflector can help.

- Rope: Extra rope is always useful, for everything from replacing a broken sheet to setting up a tow line.

- Tool Kit: There is no substitute for having a tool kit and essential spares onboard your boat.

Personal Equipment

The following personal equipment is essential as well:

- Foul-weather Gear: A good-quality rain jacket and pants are essential if you boat in a climate where rain is likely and hypothermia is a possibility. When selecting your gear, you should bend, reach, squat, and try it with a sweater underneath and a lifejacket over top to be sure it's comfortable. Opt for bright, highly visible colors.

- Lifejacket: Select one that fits well, is comfortable to move around in, and is suitable for sailing. Sailors who are out on the water frequently often opt for an inflatable lifejacket because they are most comfortable to wear.

- Safety Harness: Designed to keep you attached to the boat by a tether, a safety harness is a great addition to your personal equipment if you plan to race, sail at night, sail in more exposed waters, or sail alone. Some foul-weather gear jackets and lifejackets have them built in, which can make them easier to use.

- Sea boots and boat shoes: Dedicated sailing shoes have soft soles so they don't slip on wet decks. Keep in mind sea boots should be oversized—so if you do fall in with them on, they will come off easily.

- Sun protection: Sunglasses (polarized are preferred on the water), sun hats, long-sleeved shirts, and sunscreen are essential for sailors. With higher rates of skin cancer than the general population, we need to be especially careful about our exposure.

Don't Become a Statistic

I once asked a U.S. Coast Guard officer about what goes wrong on the water. The answer: just about everything. With an answer like that it might seem as though boating accidents are random happenings that can strike at any time. In fact, the opposite is true; boaters have an awful lot of control over their safety and well-being. And tragedies on the water are often both predictable and preventable.

 SAILOR'S WARNING

In any given year, most boating fatalities are the result of drowning—and about 84 percent of the drowning victims weren't wearing a life jacket. The U.S. Coast Guard encourages recreational boaters to make sure everyone on board wears a life jacket at all times on the water.

The U.S. Coast Guard does respond to a wide range of accidents, but the three most common mishaps in the United States are entirely predictable:

- Collision with another recreational vessel
- Collision with a fixed object
- Flooding or swamping

The preventable part of the equation is the fact that there are several basic principles of boating safety which boaters who have accidents seem to ignore, including drinking alcohol on the water, not gaining enough experience before heading out, and failing to check weather conditions such as wind, waves, and water temperature.

In an extensive survey of what types of actions led up to an accident, the U.S. Coast Guard found that alcohol and drug use, operator inattention, keeping an improper lookout, operator inexperience, rules of the road infractions, and boating in poor weather or hazardous waters topped the list.

 SAILOR'S WARNING

It might seem like boating and drinking go together—but would you pop open a beer on the highway? Drinking and driving a boat is still drinking and driving, and anyone operating a boat while under the influence of alcohol is breaking the law. Plus, thanks to the dehydrating effects of the sun, wind, and saltwater, and the rocking movement of the boat, drinking one alcoholic beverage aboard a boat is considered the equivalent to drinking three on land.

Getting Out of Trouble

Knowing how to get yourself out of trouble once you're in it is just as important as avoiding accidents. Even when assistance is coming, you should still be taking steps to help yourself. One way to prepare is to go over possible emergency situations and brainstorm ways of solving them, in advance.

Another wise plan is to make sure there is an alternate skipper onboard—someone else who can handle the boat and who can assist in an emergency. It's also important (and legally required) to make sure that all your guests know where to find and how to use the safety and communication equipment.

It's almost always better to call for assistance early on in an emergency—even if it's just to let the Coast Guard know what has occurred and what your management plan is. Recent studies show that when people put off calling for help, those emergency calls ended up being far more dangerous, for both the rescuer and victim, than they may have otherwise been.

Although the studies were land based, it makes sense that when you call for help before all hell breaks loose, it's less likely you'll end up experiencing a catastrophic cascade of failures. In fact, there are three different levels of urgency just to cover the fact that not every crisis is a matter of life and death.

A *Mayday* is called when there's imminent danger to life or to the continued viability of the vessel. But when there is no immediate urgency, boaters calling the Coast Guard should alert them to a problem by using a *Pan Pan* (danger to property or safety). *Securite* is typically called to provide safety information—such as weather updates or to alert vessels in your area that you are adrift.

Calling for Assistance

Knowing when to make the call is as important as knowing how to call. With cell phones becoming more common, people are tending to rely on them for help. (Dialing *16 will even get you the Coast Guard in some locations.) There are real problems with this type of cell phone use, though: their batteries can die, you can get out of range, and unlike a VHF radio call (where everyone in your area can hear that you need help), a cell phone call means only one person hears your call.

BETTER BOATING

If you are buying a new VHF radio, look for one that has digital selective calling (DSC). This feature provides automatic digital distress alerts, and if it's connected to a GPS, it will automatically give your position. Don't forget to obtain a Maritime Mobile Service Identity (MMSI) number for your radio to get the safety benefits from this automated system.

Having more people hear your call means there are more potential sources of assistance. There is a long tradition on the sea of boaters helping other boaters, so when recreational boaters provide assistance to each other the Coast Guard can use their limited resources for the most serious calls.

Making a VHF Radio Distress Call

Make sure your VHF radio is on, "high power" is selected, its set to Channel 16, and the volume is up so you can hear the response.

Press down the button on the microphone and call:

- Mayday. Mayday. Mayday.

- This is _____ [say vessel name three times]

- Our position is _____ [give GPS position and as much geographic reference as you can]

- The problem is _____ [briefly describe what happened—dismasted, sinking, fire, etc.]

- I require _____ [describe the assistance you require—medical help, salvage pump, tow, etc.]

- There are _____ [number] people aboard.

- They are [okay, injured, or overboard]

- [Additional details]

- Over.

Release the button and listen for a reply. Repeat every 60 seconds until you get an answer.

Stay near the radio after making a distress call—even if you know help is on its way. Often the Coast Guard will call back to clarify details or to get more information.

Managing Bad Weather

Checking the weather report doesn't guarantee perfect weather; sudden changes in the weather including squalls, rainstorms, or fog can show up unexpectedly. No one can tell you precisely what to do if you get caught out in rough conditions, but take the situation seriously. Try to head for the nearest dock or sheltered water (no need to try for your home marina if something safe is closer). If you can't make it somewhere safe, reef your sails and take the appropriate measures:

- Have everyone put on life jackets and foul-weather gear, and if you have harnesses, clip on to the boat.

- Secure all hatches and ports to keep water out.

- Secure loose gear above and below decks.

- Make sure you have your bailers, hand pumps, first aid kit, signaling devices, etc. handy.

- Double-check your position and plot it on your chart. Check for hazards you need to avoid.

- Monitor Channel 16 on your marine VHF radio for U.S. Coast Guard updates on the weather.

- Anchor the boat in a protected area that doesn't put you at risk of being blown onto a dangerous *lee shore*.

DEFINITION

A **lee shore** is a land mass that the wind is blowing on to. So if you are on your boat and the wind is blowing toward land, it would be blowing you toward a lee shore. The problem is that, as the wind blows, waves pile up and get steeper close to shore, so if you are blown toward shore you can find yourself in a surf zone and unable to maneuver through the wind and waves.

- Turn on navigation lights if visibility is reduced.

- Reduce sails further if needed and head your boat on a course that is free of hazards and is as comfortable as possible. Heave to if conditions allow.

- Turn on the engine if needed to make headway against the wind.

- In reduced visibility begin sounding one long blast on your air horn or whistle (4–6 seconds) every 2 minutes while under way and two long blasts every 2 minutes when stopped.

Getting a Tow

Despite good preparation, things can go very wrong; engines fail, your sails tear, and boats get dismasted. Or perhaps sailing conditions get to the point where it's simply quicker and safer to be towed back to safety than to sail an upwind course to safety.

In these situations you'll need to know how to be towed:

- Have the tow boat throw you the tow line from up wind.

- Attach the line around the mast with two turns and a bowline knot, unless your boat has some sort of towing fitting or bridle.

- Use plenty of line. You should use an absolute minimum of three boat lengths, but more is better. The line is also somewhat elastic, which allows it to act as a shock absorber by reducing the forces on your boat as you get towed through waves.

- Slowly have the tow boat take up the strain.

- Stay in constant communication. Either use radios or phones or work out a simple set of hand signals for slowing down, speeding up, stopping, and cutting loose.

- Center the tiller. It's important it's not turned to one side or the other unless it's time to turn.

- Keep a knife handy. You should always be ready to cut loose if you find the tow is doing damage to your boat or you feel you might hit something.

On-the-water safety is really the sum of many things; you need the boat to be prepared and you need to be personally prepared so you stay out of trouble in the first place. But you also need to know how to get help if you need it and what to do when help comes.

The Least You Need to Know

- Safe boating classes are mandatory in many states and a good way to become safer on the water. Most basic sailing classes will meet the safe boating requirement.

- Ensure that your boat has all the legally required safety gear aboard by arranging for a voluntary safety check with the U.S. Coast Guard Auxiliary.

- Additional safety equipment, including an anchor, bailer, VHF radio, sailing knife, and tool kit with spare, are not required but are wise to carry aboard.

- Personal gear is also vital safety equipment. Staying warm and comfortable or protecting yourself from the sun will help you be safe on the water.

- The U.S. Coast Guard recommends that boaters always wear a lifejacket—most drowning victims were not wearing one.

- Tie a tow line to a fitting made for towing or to the mast.

Coping with Emergencies

In This Chapter

- Getting free once you've run aground
- Stopping the flow if you're taking on water
- Knowing what to do if your engine stops
- Coping with sail or rig problems
- Putting out a fire
- Rescuing a man overboard
- Abandoning ship

One of the things you'll discover after you've sailed awhile is that sailors are very self-sufficient people. Incidents that sound like emergencies to a landlubber—running aground, taking on water, tearing a sail—simply become puzzles that need solving when you're out on the water.

Sure, you can and should call for help if you need it (and paying for a membership at a towing organization isn't a bad idea for new boaters). But the key in any crisis is to stay calm, take stock of your situation, and decide if you need assistance or if you can manage on your own. Many times you'll be able to cope on your own. Often, all that's needed is a little know-how, a good repair kit, common sense, and a bit of time.

Over the years we've gotten ourselves through just about every situation on the following list, and each time we solved a problem we gained confidence and developed new skills. So keep this in mind as you give it a try. Once you've worked your way through the problem, you'll be underway again. Then you'll be like all those other sailors you may have met—the ones who nonchalantly tell the tale of the time they lost engine power and drifted with the tide until they repaired it, or how they broke a shroud but managed to save the rig.

Running Aground

There are two types of sailors: those who run aground and those who lie. Or so goes the saying. I'm not sure if it's true or not, but I've seen an awful lot of boats run aground. The reasons are myriad. We've bumped bottom when making our way through a channel where the buoys had blown off place in a storm. Another time we dragged at anchor and ended up heeled over in the mud, waiting for high tide. We've seen other boats read the buoys wrong and drive up onto a reef. And we watched one large boat try to take a small-boat shortcut; it took a full tidal cycle for them to come free.

It's not comfortable, and you can end up with damage, but running aground isn't always the end of your sailing day(s). This boat came off safely at the next high tide.
(Evan Gatehouse)

If you've run aground, the first step is to get everyone into lifejackets and then assess the situation. Unless you are in grave danger, make sure you've put your motor in neutral, or eased sails or taken down your sails so you don't push yourself harder aground.

If you are in danger, or your boat has been damaged, or you are on a rocky or a lee shore with waves pushing you further into the beach, call the Coast Guard with a Pan Pan to advise them of your situation. You may also choose to call if it's a falling tide, late in the afternoon, or bad weather is expected.

SAILOR'S WARNING

Most people have the urge to attempt to keep going when they've run aground. The only time you should try this is if you've run aground while sailing upwind. Then try tacking over immediately by getting everyone to move to leeward side to heel the boat over as far as possible, and then, hopefully, the wind will push you back to open water.

If you're sailing downwind, or motoring, resist the urge to try to spin around and motor back out. While this may work, it could also damage your rudder.

Otherwise you probably have time to figure out what went wrong. Ask the following questions as you assess your situation:

- Is any water coming into the hull? If there is, you should deal with this issue first. You don't want to refloat a sinking boat.

- How deep is the water? Are you barely aground or well stuck?

- What is the nature of the sea bottom? If it's rocky, you should alert the Coast Guard in case you sustain damage while coming off.

- Is the tide rising or falling? A falling tide means you need to either work quickly or prepare to sit for a while. With a rising tide time may take care of the problem for you.

- Why did you go aground and where is the deeper water? Take a moment to look at your nautical chart; you don't want to end up heading into an even shallower area.

BETTER BOATING

If you have a long boat hook, you can walk around your boat and probe the bottom checking for depth and to find out what material is down there.

- Is your rudder intact? Does your steering seem to work? Assess these as best you can. If your rudder is stuck, it may be hard to tell.

If you have simply settled into sand or mud in calm conditions and think you know where the deep water is, you can probably get yourself free. If you are on a smaller boat and it's safe to do so, hopping into the water and attempting to pivot your boat so it's facing the right way is a good first step. Oh, and don't forget—if you have a centerboard or daggerboard down, try raising that first.

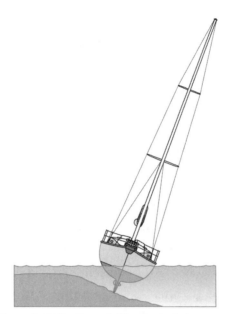

Are you still upright, or heeled well over? If you're heeled over and the tide is rising, you want to be sure that the incoming tide won't flood your boat.

Reducing Draft

Unless you're on a catamaran, every boat is deepest along the midline (where the keel is), so one of the first things you can try is to reduce your draft by heeling, or tipping, the boat over to one side to minimize the depth of keel in the water. This can be done by having everyone aboard (including the person on the wheel) shift to one side and forward (if you have a full keeled boat) and then motoring forward.

If this isn't enough, you can swing the boom out way to one side and suspend your dinghy from its end or have a few people climb out on it and hold on. The weight on the end of the boom will help heel your boat over.

Another option is to try raising sails. This can work if you have a light to moderate cross-breeze that is blowing toward deeper water. (Don't try this if the wind might blow you into a shallower area.) Raise the sails, pull the sheets in tight so you tip the boat to one side, and use your motor to get you to deeper water.

If you're still getting nowhere, try taking a halyard well out to one side, attaching it to an anchor or another boat, and pulling down. Once you've heeled the boat over, put your boat in forward, increase your speed slowly, and watch for any signs of engine overheating or decreased water flow. These are signs that the engine's cooling water intake fitting could be out of the water or that you are sucking up mud or weed through it from the bottom.

If heeling the boat over isn't helping, you can also try reducing draft by emptying water tanks (if the supply isn't critical), placing heavy gear in a dinghy, and getting everyone off the boat.

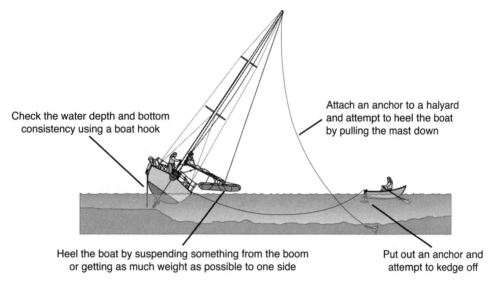

Check the water depth and bottom consistency using a boat hook

Attach an anchor to a halyard and attempt to heel the boat by pulling the mast down

Heel the boat by suspending something from the boom or getting as much weight as possible to one side

Put out an anchor and attempt to kedge off

There are several options when it comes to getting a boat off the bottom. Knowing which method to choose depends on conditions and what equipment you have available.

Kedging Off

If motoring off isn't successful, you can try *kedging off* by setting an anchor in deep water. Send your anchor out in your dinghy or another small boat (with the anchor line being paid out as the dinghy moves away from the vessel so it doesn't get caught in a propeller). Try for a minimum of 3:1 scope (the depth of water measured from the sea bottom to your deck level times 3). You can find more on anchoring in Chapter 6.

DEFINITION

Kedging off means using the anchor to pull your boat into deeper water.

If there are no other boats available and you are able to swim, you can try floating the anchor out on a PFD or fender. Swim it out to where it's to be set and carefully drop it, the more scope, the better.

When the anchor is set, try winching the boat toward it. You may need to lead the anchor line from the bow to a large winch or windlass. If you still don't budge, the anchor will hold you in place until the tide rises. If the boat is resting on a hard or rocky surface, and the tide is going to fall by more than a foot, this is a good time to put cushions and fenders under the hull to minimize damage, as your boat will continue to settle on its side as the tide drops.

SAILOR'S WARNING

Often small dinghies, power boats, or any boat with shallower draft will offer to help tow you off. But if you can't motor yourself off, chances are a smaller boat won't be successful. If a larger vessel offers, make sure they are able to maneuver in the shallow water. (You don't want two stuck boats.)

If a larger vessel offers to tow, be especially cautious when you attach the tow line. Many small boats don't have fittings that are strong enough for this purpose, and if the fitting breaks, the "elastic band" effect of the recoiling rope can be deadly. Spread the towing force out by attaching the tow rope to two bow cleats, the base of the mast or the main cockpit winches. These are all usually pretty strong points.

Taking On Water

If you notice your boat taking on water, you're going to need to find out where it's coming from and stop the flow. Assuming you haven't been in a collision (in which case you should be putting on your life jacket and calling the Coast Guard), or you haven't forgotten to put the drain plug into the back of your boat (more common than you think), chances are your leak is a slow one and you'll have time to grab a flashlight and go hunt it down.

If it's a fast leak, call for help immediately (see Chapter 7 for more on how to make distress calls) and, if you are otherwise safe, begin making your way back to shore. Meanwhile:

- Have everyone put on a life jacket.

- Start your bilge pumps. If you are using a manual bilge pump, assign someone to bail the water while you look for the leak.

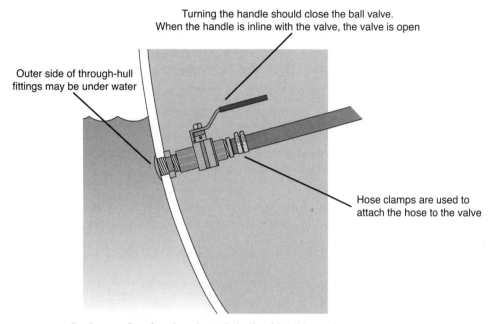

Turning the handle should close the ball valve.
When the handle is inline with the valve, the valve is open

Outer side of through-hull
fittings may be under water

Hose clamps are used to
attach the hose to the valve

Leaks are often found at through-hull valves. It's prudent to carry extra hose clamps as well as cone-shaped wooden bungs, which can be hammered into damaged through-hulls.

- Check the through-hulls. If you have recently worked on any plumbing or had engine maintenance done, start in those places first. Forgotten, loose, or broken hose clamps are often the culprit. If this is the case, close the sea cock and reattach the hose clamps, then reopen the seacock.

- Check the engine hoses. A burst hose in either the engine's cooling or exhaust system could be the issue. You can trim off the damaged bit of hose (the engine needs to be turned off, of course) and reattach it.

  If you don't have the supplies, a leaking water hose can be given a short-term repair by wrapping it in plastic wrap to seal the leak and then binding it with electrical or duct tape to hold the wrap in place. Another option is to fit a section of larger spare hose over the leak and secure it with hose clamps.

- Check your keel bolts or centerboard housing. If this is the source, and the water seepage is manageable, wait until you have returned to the dock to arrange a repair.

- Look at the stuffing box on the propeller and rudder shafts. A small amount of dripping is normal, but if the water is streaming you can attempt to tighten the *stuffing box* nut by a half a turn. (You should have a repair manual on hand before attempting this.) Stuffing boxes use a large nut, so slip joint pliers or a small pipe wrench may be necessary.

DEFINITION

A **stuffing box** is an assembly found on propeller or rudder shafts that holds a seal that prevents leaks between sliding or turning parts.

- Taste the water. If it's fresh you may have a leak in the boat's fresh water system. If this is the case, shut off the water pump or see if you can track it to the source.

If you still can't track down the leak, have one more search around with your flashlight, then head back to the dock for assistance. Never leave a boat with an undiagnosed leak unattended at the dock; it may sink while you are away.

Engine Problems

You're adrift in light wind 4 miles from the dock, everyone's hungry, hot, and tired and the engine won't start. I know, I know—you have a sailboat, so you adjust your sails and make your slow way in. Most of the time that works, but sometimes if the wind is too light, the current is against you, or heavy traffic makes maneuvering by sail difficult you need the engine. One option is to call for a tow (this is not a Coast Guard moment unless you're in danger), but before you do that, it's worth troubleshooting your engine for a few of the more common issues that you only need basic know-how to fix.

Remember to leave someone on deck to keep an eye out for other boats and alert them to your inability to maneuver as you work though the problem.

BETTER BOATING

Running out of gas is the number one reason that boaters call for a tow. So even if you plan to sail all day and only use the engine to maneuver at the dock, make sure you carry enough fuel to motor home plus a bit more, just in case the wind doesn't cooperate.

Lost Power

Problem: The engine sputtered and then lost power.

Diagnosis: You may have a clogged fuel filter.

Solution: Change the fuel filter. If you don't have a spare, you can remove the one you have and empty the housing of any water or debris. However, if the filter itself is clogged with gunk, this probably won't help.

Prevention: Filter your fuel as it comes aboard. If you are going to leave your boat for any length of time, always fill the tank so condensation can't form.

Supplies needed: Spare filter and a filter wrench.

Overheating

Problem: The high temperature light or alarm is on, or you smell a hot engine.

Diagnosis: A hot engine usually means that something has gone wrong with the cooling system. If you have an outboard motor, see if the telltale stream of water is spurting from the bottom of the outboard cowling. If it isn't, shut the engine down immediately to prevent damage. For inboard engines, look over the side of the boat where the exhaust is coming out. There should be a mixture of water and exhaust gases. If there's no cooling water coming out, shut the engine down and find out why.

Solution: Look for an obstruction in the raw water intake or filter, such as weeds, mud, or a plastic bag (check outside the boat where the water is sucked in as well as on the inboard side of the system). Also check for a burst or split hose.

There's also a chance the cooling water pump impeller (the small rubber rotating part inside the pump that moves the water) has failed. With outboard motors, you can't change this impeller on the water. But with inboard boat engines, impellers are easy to change if you have a spare impeller, a wrench to remove the pump from its bracket (if needed), and a screwdriver to remove the pump cover plate.

Dead Engine

Problem: The engine won't crank when you turn the key.

Diagnosis: This may be caused by a low or dead battery, or it could be a loose wire.

Solution: Switch to the starting battery; you may have drained the house battery, but hopefully you have a second battery in the system. Check the wiring behind the kill switch and the starter key itself. Then check the wiring on the starter motor and at the battery itself. Look for a loose wire connection or obvious corrosion.

Prevention: If your wiring is in poor condition, have it replaced.

Supplies needed: Screwdrivers, multimeter, and a crescent wrench.

Problem: The engine died suddenly.

Solution: Check to see if someone bumped the kill switch and then check to see if you're out of fuel; after that, look for a loose connection or corroded switch.

Bad Vibration

Problem: The engine and boat are vibrating in an unusual manner.

Solution: Something might be caught on the propeller. Turn off the engine and see if you snagged a fishing line, kelp, or some sort of garbage. Use a boathook and knife to remove it.

Tools and Spares to Have on Hand

Many common engine problems can be avoided with regular maintenance. But if you're going to be boating regularly, make sure you have your engine's manual and a good repair reference book as well as a range of tools and spares. Also consider taking a basic engine maintenance course.

Make sure your tools are in a plastic toolbox and give them an occasional squirt with some anticorrosion spray to keep them rust free.

Here is a list of basic tools and spares you should always have on hand.

Basic Tools:

- 1-lb. ball peen hammer
- Combination wrenches (metric for most engines and inch (SAE) to suit the nuts and bolts for fasteners all over the boat)
- Allen Keys
- Crescent (adjustable) wrench
- Electrical multimeter
- Multibit screwdriver
- Needlenose pliers
- Vise-grip

Basic Spares:

- An assortment of stainless steel nuts, bolts, and screws are often available as kits in marine chandleries (shops selling nautical items for ships and boats).

- Bulbs for interior lights and navigation lights

- Dacron sail repair tape

- Duct tape

- Electrical tape

- Engine-cooling water hose

- Engine fuel filter

- Engine oil and oil filter

- Engine V-belts for alternator and water pump

- Fuses

- Hose clamps in various sizes

- Rope—a few 6-foot lengths of $\frac{1}{4}$-inch rope as a minimum, and some lighter cord for temporary lashings

- Shackles and pulleys, a few, sized similarly to the fittings on your mast and rigging

- Spark plugs (outboard motors)

- Waterproof flashlight

- Water pump impeller

- WD-40

Torn Sails and Other Rig Damage

Sails, sheets, halyards, shrouds, and stays can last for years without showing too many signs of wear. And unless you're getting them inspected regularly, damage can sneak up on you. With sails, one common reason they get damaged is *chafe*, when they are allowed to rub against something. Sun, salt, and dirt also weaken sail fabric and stitching, causing sails to tear when they are exposed to sudden high winds. A common way to tear a sail is to overtension it.

Sail Damage

If you tear a sail, the most important thing to do is to stop using it immediately. If you still need the sail in order to get home, you can try lowering it or reefing it so that the damaged area is taken out of service. Another way to make an emergency repair is to use adhesive Dacron tape on both sides of the tear. Most sailmakers recommend at least 2-inch-wide sections of tape for best results, and the sail and tape have to be dry.

This isn't a permanent fix. Sail tape only works in low-stress areas and even then it's typically stitched over. But the tape could get you home so you can get your sails to a sailmaker.

Sheets and Halyards

When it comes to sheets and halyards breaking, again, the most important thing is to get the sail down or under control so no further damage can be done. Flapping sails, called luffing, can wear out a sail quickly. A broken halyard is a difficult item to fix at sea, so if you have a spare halyard, you can try using that. Otherwise you are going to need to make it home under one sail.

Sheets should be easier to repair and can be used in their shortened state; simply tie the sheet back on to wherever it broke or chafed through.

Broken Shrouds and Stays

Broken standing rigging is potentially the most dangerous of rigging breakdowns, because those wires are what are keeping your mast standing. When a mast wire breaks, the violent motion of the wire can do damage to people and equipment and the lost support can topple your mast. A toppled mast is a dangerous and ultimately expensive situation. The mast and boom can do harm to people, damage or hole your boat, and a downed mast almost always destroys your sails.

The key is to act quickly, in the hope you can re-support your mast before it falls. If a side shroud breaks, you need to immediately take the pressure off the broken side by getting it to leeward. This normally means tacking.

The next step is to replace it as best you can. Typically the best option will be to lower the mainsail and move the main halyard to a cleat or other strong point near the chainplate and then tension it on a winch. You won't be sailing home, but you may keep your mast up.

If your forestay breaks, release some of the pressure on the mast by immediately heading down wind. But don't ease the jib halyard or the main sheet; these may be keeping the mast up and keeping it from falling backward.

If you have a spinnaker halyard, you can move that to a bow cleat or another strong point and tension it to help support the mast.

If the backstay breaks, head into the wind quickly to relieve pressure on the mast and keep it from falling forward. Then lower the mainsail and move the main halyard to the stern of the boat and tension it.

In all these cases a Pan Pan call to the Coast Guard to alert them to your situation may be in order.

Fire Aboard

Fire is one emergency that sailors rightly fear. When you're on a boat, there's no place to escape the smoke and flames except off the boat. By having the right fire extinguishers aboard, you'll be able to fight a small fire effectively (if it's safe to do so).

It's a good idea to locate extinguishers close to possible fire sources, such as the galley stove and the engine compartment. It's also a good idea to have one extinguisher close to the cabin entrance; that way you can grab it and point it into the cabin to help fight the fire. Keep in mind that the Coast Guard requirements for fire extinguishers (boats under 26' are only required to have one) are a minimum requirement. We like to carry an extra two.

SAILOR'S WARNING

Fire extinguishers need maintenance. Twice a year (daylight savings time changes are a good reminder), turn over your fire extinguisher and firmly pound the bottom with a rubber hammer a few times. This will prevent the dry powder in the extinguisher from becoming packed tightly by the boat's motion and will ensure it's ready to go in an emergency. When inverting the extinguisher, place it next to your ear and you can hear the contents slide downward. Check the pressure gauge regularly to make sure the extinguisher hasn't lost its charge. Your boat insurance may require the extinguishers to be regularly checked or professionally serviced.

Fight a fire as you would on land—by aiming the extinguisher at the base of the flames and sweeping the nozzle back and forth. Because you're on a boat, however, you'll have a few extra steps to take. You should call the Coast Guard as soon as possible because fire aboard is a Mayday situation. If possible, you should also change your course and sail down wind to keep the flames in the cabin. But be sure to aim away from other vessels and do not bring a burning boat into a marina where it could cause other vessels to burn. Have everyone aboard don life jackets and prepare themselves to abandon ship.

If the fire is in a sealed engine compartment, open the door or lid just enough to get the extinguisher nozzle inside and then discharge it. You're trying not to add more oxygen to the fire.

Boats with inboard engines should have an automatically activated fire extinguisher in the engine compartment. Opening the engine compartment can cause the dramatic flare-up. Another option is to have a fire port—a small covered opening that is only used in the event of a fire.

If you suspect the fire is electrical (you're seeing sparks or arcing), turn off the main battery switch immediately. And be sure to replace all suspect wires before turning the battery back on.

Don't forget that buckets of water are easily available if a wood interior is burning, but you never fight an oil- (diesel or gasoline) or electrical-based fire with water. Be prepared to abandon ship if the fire gets out of control. Keep in mind this can happen very quickly on a fiberglass boat.

Man Overboard

If you sail, one of the things you'll need to practice again and again is a man overboard drill. Practice it in all conditions. Do them as surprises for your crew. Do them by yourself. Try throwing something small in the water, like a coconut, which resembles a head, and discover how hard it is to see it. Then try pulling people aboard your boat when they offer no help.

Once you've done a few of these drills, and learned just how difficult it is to find and recover something you've dropped in the water yourself, you'll come to the sobering conclusion that falling overboard is more than an inconvenience, it's a life-threatening situation.

Learning to perform a man overboard procedure is essential. There are seven steps to every man overboard. They are:

1. Alert the crew.

2. Get buoyancy to the victim.

   3. Keep the victim in sight.

   4. Return to the victim quickly.

   5. Connect the victim to the boat.

   6. Get the victim back on board.

   7. Call the Coast Guard.

Step 1: Alert the Crew

As soon as someone goes over, whoever witnesses the accident should yell "Man overboard!" so everyone is alert (and boats that are near you hear). If you have a man overboard pole with a flag, toss it in as near to the person as possible. (But it's not a harpoon, so don't spear the victim either.)

Step 2: Get Buoyancy to the Victim

Get buoyancy to the victim by throwing something such as a life jacket to them. You may be required by the Coast Guard to have a type IV throwable device handy, but an even better plan than throwing the typical square cushion (which is often found stuffed in a locker or under the captain's backside) is to make sure everyone on your boat is already wearing a life jacket. Other great options are life rings or rescue collars that are attached to the boat by a line. But keep in mind if you are sailing away from a victim you may be pulling the rescue device away with you.

A few words about PFDs: Most drowning victims were within sight of a rescuer and may have been saved if they were wearing a Personal Floatation Device (PFD). Every sailor should own a floatation device that fits well and is comfortable; in other words, one you'll wear.

When selecting one, look for one with less restrictive arm holes and that fits snugly but not tightly. Make sure you can sit comfortably and move around freely. It's too big if you can pull it over your ears, and too small if you can't fasten it easily. And choose something that's a bright color; the idea is to be visible.

Inflatable PFD's, that either inflate automatically when immersed in water, or manually by the wearer, tend to be the most comfortable and nonrestrictive option and are popular with sailors. But they're not approved for those under 16 years of age.

Step 3: Keep the Victim in Sight

When you hear, "Man overboard!" you should assign one person (not the person driving the boat) the task of pointing to the victim. The only way you are going to keep track of someone in the water is for one person to keep their eyes on them. People are very hard to see in the water and if your victim was injured or unconscious when they went in, they are not going to be able to wave you down.

Most marine GPS devices have a man overboard button (MOB). If you have enough crew, order someone to push it as soon as possible to mark the victim's position. At night this can give you a place to begin searching. But in daylight, keeping an eye on the person in the water is a bigger priority.

BETTER BOATING

In a perfect rescue, everything should happen in an orderly, almost simultaneous way. Staying calm and making sure you don't make things worse is important.

Step 4: Return to the Victim Quickly

The next step is to get back to the victim. There are loads of complicated figure-eight maneuvers and other such things taught by sailing schools, which are meant to get you back to the victim quickly and safely. The thing is, every boat and every situation is going to be different.

The goal is to turn the boat back around quickly and sail back to the victim while keeping them in sight. If sailing away and returning suits conditions, do that. Turn on the engine (even if you don't need it, it's good to have it on) but keep it in neutral because if you throw the person a life ring or rescue collar, you will have lines in the water and don't want to stall the engine by tangling the propeller in them.

Head up and tack the boat so you are approaching the victim from the windward side. As you get close, luff the sails to slow the boat. You want to approach slowly so you don't sail past the victim, and you want to be cautious, so you don't hit them.

The crash stop may be the fastest and safest way to get back to a victim—especially if you don't have a full crew because you just lost one overboard. The crash stop is exactly what it sounds like: you stop immediately. Practice it to make sure you understand the process. Ideally you'll tack and heave-to (see Chapter 4 for heaving-to) and still be close enough to assist your victim.

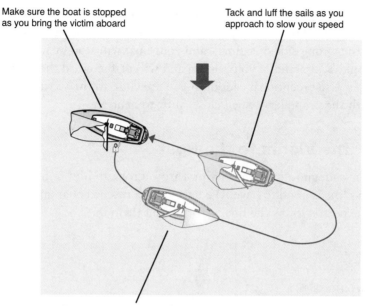

Make sure the boat is stopped as you bring the victim aboard

Tack and luff the sails as you approach to slow your speed

Sail away and prepare to tack while having crew keep an eye on the victim

Sail away on a beam reach. Tack as soon as you are able and return to the victim on a close reach. Luff up into the wind as you approach.

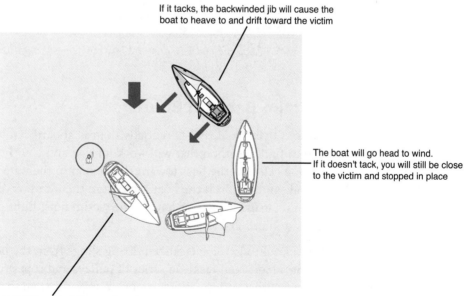

If it tacks, the backwinded jib will cause the boat to heave to and drift toward the victim

The boat will go head to wind. If it doesn't tack, you will still be close to the victim and stopped in place

As soon as someone has fallen overboard, put the tiller hard over to leeward

Stopping immediately might be the best choice, especially if you are short-handed.

To perform a crash stop, push the tiller hard to leeward or turn the wheel so you head up and tack. Don't adjust the sails, though. The jib should backwind, with the wind blowing on the wrong side of the sail, and your boat will stop by heaving-to. At this point you should be upwind of your victim and will drift toward them. If needed, motor a little closer. Use exceptional caution if you are close to the victim so as to not run over them with the propeller—when close, shift to neutral.

Step 5: Connect the Victim to the Boat

If you are not close enough to grab the victim, throw a rope to him or her. Some sort of buoyant heaving line is good to have. We have both a rescue collar and life ring on our boat. Once the person grabs the line, start pulling them in.

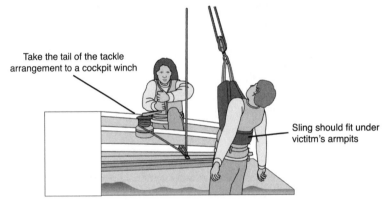

Take the tail of the tackle arrangement to a cockpit winch

Sling should fit under victitm's armpits

Hoisting someone with a block and tackle is often the only way to get them aboard.

Step 6: Get the Victim Back on Board

Getting someone who is tired, cold, and potentially injured aboard can be tricky, and you're going to need to find a method that will work for you and your boat. If you have low freeboard, you can heel the boat toward the person in the water and pull them up to the gunwale and then roll the boat away from them to sort of scoop them aboard. But don't plan on using ladders or having the victim hoist him- or herself up; these methods are just too unreliable.

Many people find it helpful to lower specialized lifting slings from the boom and hoist up a victim using a block and tackle (a series of pulleys and ropes). Most slings and rescue collars come with a variety of directions, so find a system that will work on your boat and then test it before you need it.

Step 7: Call the Coast Guard

The seventh step in rescuing a man overboard would be calling the Coast Guard. This can actually happen at any moment a crewmember can safely call. But make sure that calling the Coast Guard doesn't hamper the actual rescue. Assign the task to someone who isn't actively spotting, steering, or handling sails. If your victim becomes hypothermic, you will need to actively warm them or call for help.

After you call you may discover you don't need the Coast Guard. If that's the case just call them back and let them know the emergency has passed. But it's good to know help is on its way if you have a medical emergency or are unable to locate your man overboard.

Abandon Ship

There are really very few situations when you should have to leave your boat. These include a fire that can't be contained, or your boat sinking because of a major leak. The sailor's rule of thumb is that you should only step up from your sinking vessel into a dinghy or life raft. In other words, don't leave the boat until you absolutely have to.

SAILOR'S WARNING

One reason not to abandon ship unless you absolutely have to is that abandoning ship is not without its own risks. Abandoned sailboats are often recovered later on, still afloat. The crews would have been safer aboard.

If you need to abandon ship, follow these steps:

- Put on any available foul-weather clothing, including gloves and headgear. Put on your lifejackets if they are not already on.

- Make a Mayday call on your VHF before leaving the boat. If you already have a Mayday call in, let the Coast Guard know you are abandoning your boat. Give your position by either reading the GPS position or giving a reference a geographical position such as "½ mile North of Windsor Point," providing the number of people leaving the boat, and saying whether you have a dinghy or you're getting into the water. If you have an *EPIRB* or *PLB*, turn it on and bring it with you.

- Take a handheld VHF if you have one, cell phone, flares, a whistle, and a flashlight, because you want to have means of attracting a rescuer's attention.

DEFINITION

EPIRB stands for Emergency Position Indicating Radio Beacon, a radio distress beacon. **PLB** stands for Personal Locator Beacon, a distress beacon similar to an EPIRB, but smaller and with shorter battery life.

- Get into your dinghy or life raft without getting into the water if possible. Get a safe distance from the sinking or burning boat.

- Huddle together for warmth and stay low in the dinghy to keep it stable.

- Don't use flares until there is a real chance of them being seen by rescuers.

SAILOR'S WARNING

Each season when you check to see if your flares are still current (they are only valid for 4 years), give yourself a refresher course on how to use them:

- In an emergency, aerial flares should be shot into the wind at a bit of an angle, not straight up. In a strong wind, lower the angle to about 45 degrees.
- Handheld flares should be held on the downwind side of your boat and body. Don't look directly into the flare.

The Least You Need to Know

- If you run aground and it's safe to do so, the first step is to assess the situation before trying to get free.
- Taking on water is a common emergency. If the leak is a slow one, get the bilge pump running and then track down the source of the leak.
- If your engine won't start and you're in a safe situation, it may be worth troubleshooting before you call for help.
- You should never attempt to sail with a torn sail—it will likely tear further.
- If a rigging wire breaks, the first step is to take the pressure off of it by tacking or changing course; the next step is to replace it as best you can.
- Maintain your fire extinguishers, place them strategically throughout the boat, and consider carrying a couple more than the Coast Guard–recommended minimum.
- Practicing man overboard drills is an essential part of sailing. You should make a plan for getting buoyancy to the person in the water, keeping them in sight, getting back to them, and getting them aboard.
- Abandon boat only if you have no choice.

Getting Where You're Going

Ships are the nearest thing to dreams that hands have ever made.

—Robert N. Rose, Author

Once you have some of the mechanics of sailing down, it's time to think about going somewhere. Navigation has changed dramatically over the past few years. Know that GPS you have in your car? There's also a version of that for your boat.

In Part 3 you learn to use and read traditional paper charts, but you also learn about your electronic options as well as the rules of the road, which explain who has right of way in various situations.

This part will also pull together a few useful boating skills, including how to determine which knots to use in which situations (and how to tie them), how to maintain your boat in an eco-friendly way, and how to decide what should be in your tool box. And assuming that you haven't got a boat yet but are thinking about getting one, you learn how to choose the right boat for right now, and discover all the steps in shopping for, testing, and buying a boat.

Paper Navigating

In This Chapter

- Gathering the right tools and publications
- Reading a chart
- Finding your position
- Plotting a course

Several years ago my husband and I were the first to arrive in a harbor where we planned to meet friends for a weekend on the water. After consulting the chart, we chose a good area to drop our anchor and then watched our friends come in. A few minutes later, they prepared to anchor in an area that our chart indicated had fouled ground (a sea bottom unsuitable for anchoring due to a hazard of some sort).

We called over on the VHF radio to alert them and learned that while they had a chart for the harbor, they didn't have a *Chart No. 1: Chart Symbols, Abbreviations, and Terms*, the 100+ page listing that provides a key to the hundreds of details found on a nautical chart. They were surprised to learn that the area outlined by a dotted line was not highlighting a "good place to anchor" as they had guessed, but instead indicated a spot where they could easily have snagged and lost their anchor on old logging debris.

A typical coastal chart contains a tremendous amount of information, but learning how to decipher the various symbols and illustrations is just the beginning of coastal navigation. This chapter highlights a few essential publications you should have aboard and describes a couple of basic piloting skills, but consider taking a basic coastal navigation course if you're going to spend much time on the water.

The Tools of Navigation

The basic tools of navigation haven't changed much in the past few hundred years of sea travel. And unless you plan to go with a few of the high-tech options, the contents of your chart table might not look that different than Captain Cook's. Navigational tools can be grouped by use. You'll have your chart, of course, then you'll have two sets of tools: one set for gathering information about your location, speed, and direction of travel; and another set for locating (or plotting) this information onto a chart.

With a chart and a few basic navigation instruments, you'll be able to navigate safely in coastal areas.

You'll also need a few books and publications. While great guidebooks can be found in nautical bookstores and chandleries, many official publications are available to download for free from the appropriate government agency. (Keep in mind that while navigation is similar worldwide, your specific country or region will have its own publications. Check Appendix B for a listing of some of the available publications.

Basic Navigating Tools

Here are the basic navigating tools you'll need to become familiar with:

- *Compass:* A steering compass allows you to maintain a course in relation to a compass direction (as opposed to wind direction). Most are found mounted on a binnacle (a center console housing the ship's compass and other navigation instruments) or on a bulkhead, where they can be read easily from the tiller or wheel position. In addition to digital compasses, which are becoming increasingly popular and provide easy-to-understand readouts, most boats also use traditional compasses.

- *Handheld Compass:* A hand-bearing compass helps you determine the direction an object is relative to you and fulfills a different role than a mounted compass. It's useful for avoiding collisions, confirming your exact location, or for measuring how far off a point you are. Digital compasses cost a bit more but are easier to use than traditional hockey puck–style compasses.

BETTER BOATING

Looking for a smartphone app to make compass reading easier? Compass Eye offers a real-time compass that's overlaid on top of your smartphone's camera view to provide a bearing. The app also works on tablets.

- *Clock:* There is a reason boats used to come with a ship's clock (and not just so a sailor knew when his *watch* ended). An accurate timepiece also lets you know how long it takes to get somewhere. With that information you can determine your distance traveled if you know your speed.

- *Fish Finding Depth Sounder:* Most of us use our depth sounders (often in the form of fish finders) to keep an eye out for shoaling or underwater dangers, or to calculate how much scope to put out when anchoring, but they have another use. Knowing how deep the water is can help you determine your position when you compare it with the depths noted on a chart.

- *Knotmeter:* Think of a knotmeter as a marine speedometer. It will display the speed (in knots) of your boat moving through the water. What it can't show is your speed relative to the ground you're covering underwater. If there is a current (either with or against you), the knotmeter won't give you this information, either.

- *Mathematical Dividers:* Don't worry, the math isn't complicated, despite the fact dividers may bring back memories of school. Used to measure distance on a chart, they work by opening up the span of the moveable legs, measuring a plotted course, and then checking the distance against the latitude scale.

- *Protractor:* Navigational protractors come in a variety of forms. The square Douglas protractor is one popular model. It's useful for setting a course and finding your positions.

- *Parallel Rulers:* Another tool for plotting the direction of a course, the parallel ruler uses the chart's compass rose to determine the compass course you need to steer to get to your destination. They can be walked across a chart by hinging and unhinging the two pieces.

- *Binoculars:* Useful for identifying buoys and landmarks. Some even come with a built-in compass.

BETTER BOATING

Make sure your chart table also contains a couple of pencils, a pencil sharpener, and a good quality eraser. Often when double-checking a course, you'll find things you need to change, and if you're using the same chart over and over, you may want to erase old routes to avoid confusion.

Basic Navigating Books and Publications

Here are the basic books and publications you'll need to become familiar with:

- *Chart No. 1: Nautical Chart Symbols, Abbreviations and Terms*, is a free 100+ page book that is available in nautical bookstores or for download from NOAA at nauticalcharts.noaa.gov/mcd/chartno1.htm in the United States or from charts.gc.ca/publications/chart1-carte1/index-eng.asp in Canada.

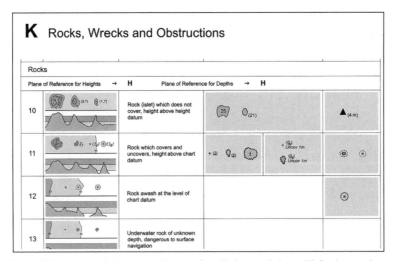

Chart No. 1 acts as a key or dictionary for all the symbols you'll find on a chart. They are grouped according to type to make them easy to locate.

(NOAA)

- *Notices to Mariners:* Information notices, including changes to charts and new hazards or obstructions, are published weekly and can be found at navcen. uscg.gov/?pageName=lnmMain

- *Coast Pilots (US) or Sailing Directions (Canada):* Designed for commercial ships, these official publications still contain valuable navigational information for recreational boaters. They can be found at nauticalcharts.noaa.gov/nsd/ cpdownload.htm in the United States or charts.gc.ca/publications/sd-in/sd-in-eng.asp in Canada.

- *Tide and Current Tables:* Available each year from your local marine store, online, or from NOAA's website. You should have these on hand to consult when needed. (See Chapter 3 for more information.)

- *Collision Regulations:* While it's useful (and important!) to memorize who the *give way vessel* is and who the *stand on vessel* is in every situation, having some sort of cheat sheet or even a more detailed book available is good practice. (See Chapter 10 for more information.)

DEFINITION

The **give way vessel** is the vessel designated to alter its course and speed when a collision is possible. The **stand-on vessel** is the one designated to maintain its course and speed when a collision is possible.

- *Aids to Navigation System:* Was it "red, right, returning"? And what exactly does a black and yellow buoy mean again? Unlike road signs, navigational markers are not always self-explanatory, and having a book to consult can be a great help. (See Chapter 10 for more information.)

Chart Basics

So now you have all this stuff and you're wondering what the heck you're supposed to do with it. The first thing you'll want to do is become familiar with how to read a chart, before you need one. Like a road map, a chart is a large piece of paper that when unfolded is a visual representation of a section of the earth's surface. But unlike a road map, a chart emphasizes details and features on the wet side of a shoreline.

Title Block

The location of the title block will vary from chart to chart, but once you find it you'll see it contains important information about what area the chart covers, what measurements are used, and any important notes or cautions that the chart user should be aware of.

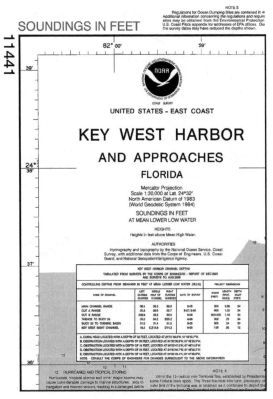

The title block shows that this is a Key West Harbor chart
and that the soundings are measured in feet.
(NOAA)

Make a special note of the sounding datum. Your chart will show soundings in feet, soundings in meters, or soundings in fathoms (1 fathom = 6 ft.). For example, let's say you see a depth marking of *2* on your chart. For safe sailing, you'll need to know whether the chart datum shows feet (2 ft.), meters ($6\frac{1}{2}$ ft.), or fathoms (12 ft.) for safe sailing.

Latitude and Longitude

The fact that maps are attempting to represent a three-dimensional object on a flat surface is something chart makers have tried to address by developing different projections. The most common representation used for nautical charts is a Mercator projection. The reason I mention this is because on a Mercator chart, the *latitude* scale (found on the vertical sides of the chart) is where we measure distance.

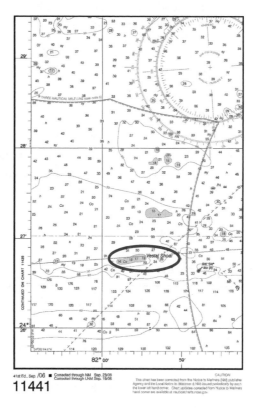

The latitude scale is found up both sides of the chart; the longitude scale is found along the top and bottom.
(NOAA)

The way it works is 1 minute of latitude (say the distance from 24°26' to 24°27' shown on this chart) equals 1 nautical mile. Each degree is divided into 60 minutes, and each minute has 60 seconds. Don't try this on the *longitude* scale though, because the distance between minutes of longitude decreases as you move closer to the poles.

To locate a position, you use the latitude and longitude lines as a grid. The shallow patch called Vestal Shoal on the image above is located at roughly 24°26.75'N, 81°59.5'W.

> **DEFINITION**
>
> The **longitude** is a geographical coordinate that indicates how far east or west you are from the Prime Meridian (Greenwich, England). The **latitude** is a north/south coordinate that indicates how far north or south you are from the equator. The intersection of latitude and longitude will indicate exactly where you are on Earth. For example, the Golden Gate Bridge is located at 37°49'N and 122°29'W.

Scale

The scale of a chart is the ratio between distance represented on a chart and the actual distance it represents. For example, a 1:20,000 scale means anything shown on the chart is actually 20,000 times larger in real life. Charts come in a variety of scales, but in relative terms a *small scale chart* shows small amount of detail and covers a large area, while a *large scale chart* shows large amounts of detail and covers a small area.

Selecting the Correct Chart

Chart Type	From	To	Description
Harbor and Approach	1:5,000	1:30,000	Charts used to approach confined waters or for harbors and anchorages
Coastal	1:30,000	1:150,000	Used for inshore navigation such as large bays or for coastal areas requiring more detail
Offshore or Planning	150,000	1:6,000,000	Offshore voyaging or planning a longer trip

Charts often show the same area at different scales, so it is important to select charts based on how you will be using them.

Chart Details

Some chart details are self-evident while others are more easily deciphered using Chart No. 1.

On the following chart, you'll see wrecks near Wisteria Island, a spoil area (an area where dumping has occurred, usually from dredging) indicated by the dotted line around Tank Island and multiple navigational buoys marking a channel.

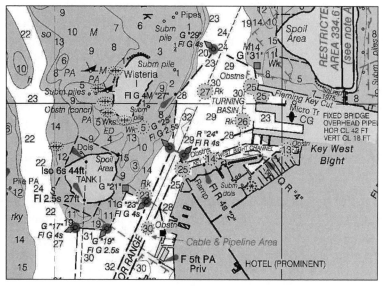

Key West Harbor chart showing a wide range of details.

While the amount of information can seem overwhelming, keep in mind the detail is provided so you know where you are and how to safely get to where you want to go. To do this you'll want to note and understand the water depths, the location of submerged hazards, and the meaning of navigational aids. Symbols showing a prominent hotel, a fixed bridge, and various piers are to help you orient yourself.

Using a Compass

Before you get too far into navigating, you're going to need to get proficient at reading a compass and steering a compass course. It works this way: after plotting a course on your chart or on your GPS, you'll get a compass course to steer, say, 165 degrees.

So holding the wheel, you'll look at the steering compass. A compass is divided into 360 increments: north is 000 degrees, east is 090 degrees, south is 180 degrees, and west is 270 degrees. If you are currently steering south, or 180 degrees, you are going to be altering your course about 15 degrees to port, until the bow of the boat and the lubber line on the compass (the fixed vertical post indicating the front of the compass) lines up with 165 degrees. Once you have that heading, adjust your sails and then get the hang of steering the course.

Steering a compass course isn't as simple as it might seem—don't expect to hold the course in a rock-steady way. Most people find that rather than staring intently at the compass number (which will bounce around, not matter how good you are), it's easier to find a landmark on shore, or some other shape on the horizon to steer toward (just don't pick a ship in motion). If you're steering straight into the sea, with no landmarks available, aim for an average 5 degrees off on either side of your goal.

Try practicing steering and altering compass courses before you're actually heading somewhere specific. And keep in mind that steering a compass course can be more tiring than simply sailing for fun, so be sure to switch off with another crew member as needed.

Another use of the compass is to take bearings. A simple way to take a compass bearing is a bow-on bearing. If you have the space and maneuverability, aim your bow at a landmark or an object and read the numbers on the compass. This resulting reading is your magnetic compass bearing.

SAILOR'S WARNING

Wondering if you are on a collision course with another vessel? Your handheld compass lets you keep track of the *relative bearing* of the other boat. If their bearing doesn't change, you are on a collision course.

- As soon as you see a vessel that concerns you, take a compass reading on it with your hand-bearing compass.
- Take a second reading after an interval (2 minutes if you are close, 5 minutes if more distant).
- If the two bearings are the same, you are on a collision course and should follow the rules of the road for your situation (Chapter 10).

It's more typical to take a bearing with a handheld compass. But getting a consistent reading from a handheld compass can take a bit of practice. These bearings are taken by holding the compass close to your eye and looking at the number on the compass and the bearing object simultaneously. Be sure to keep a pencil and paper handy to jot down the number you saw.

True North and Magnetic North

What does a compass do? Well, it helps you figure out which way you're going by pointing to north. But which north? That's not a trick question; there are two norths in navigation, true north (the geometric north pole at 90°N latitude, right at the top of the earth where Santa lives), and the magnetic north pole, where your compass actually points to. As of 2012 the magnetic north pole is around 85°N, somewhere in northern Canada. (The magnetic north pole drifts around a bit, but it's a slow change.)

When you plot bearings or courses on a chart, you need to know if the course is true north or magnetic north. The difference in angle between where your compass points to (magnetic north) and true north is called the variation. To add a bit of complication to your navigating, the variation changes from place to place. For example, in San Francisco Bay, variation is about 14°E, but in the Chesapeake Bay it's 11°W.

Because the magnetic north pole drifts around, variation also changes slightly with time. If you look at the *compass rose* printed on the chart of your local area, you'll see that the inner compass bearings point to magnetic north, and this variation will be listed. Below it will be the amount it changes in a year.

For example, on our San Francisco chart compass rose it says "VAR 14°30'E (2009)" and below it is listed "ANNUAL DECREASE 6'". So in 2013 you'll have to adjust the variation slightly from the printed value. The year 2013 is 4 years from 2009, so the total decrease in variation is 4 years × 6' each year = 24'. So the variation in 2013 will be 14°30' (the 2009 value) decreased by 24' = 14°06'. That's close enough to 14°E for navigation purposes.

BETTER BOATING

When you're navigating, rounding off to the nearest degree is appropriate. Most people can only steer a compass course +/–5 degrees anyway.

There is one other change to where the compass points that you need to know. It's the error due to the boat's local magnetic field. Things like loudspeakers, handheld VHFs, and other items with magnetic fields can affect it. So can putting any good-sized steel object near your compass. It will vary depending on which way the boat is pointing. This error is called *deviation*, and it's usually only a few degrees. It varies with the direction the boat is pointing.

Measuring Your Boat's Deviation and Adjusting the Compass

If you're lucky, a previous owner of the boat will have measured the deviation and listed it for you on a card. Or a new boat may have it done. But this isn't commonly done unless the vessel is a commercial ship or a good-sized yacht. You can hire a professional compass adjuster to do this, but it's not too hard to do yourself. The details of doing so are beyond the scope of this chapter, but there are lots of articles online giving directions. With the use of GPS, it is sadly pretty common for many boat owners not to bother with it as the errors are usually small. But this could be a mistake if your GPS dies and you're trying to find your way home with just the compass.

Hand-bearing compasses usually show small amounts of deviation which can be ignored if you use them away from any magnetic fields caused by metal on your boat.

Getting Your Bearings

Getting your bearings in a literal sense means figuring out where you are in relation to other things. These days most sailors use a GPS (Global Positioning System) to find their position. At its most simple, a GPS uses satellite signals to give you your position as a set of latitude and longitude numbers that you can then transfer onto a chart to find your location (more on using a GPS in Chapter 10). But even with all the high-tech gadgets sailors have available to them, learning to navigate with old-school tools is still an essential safety skill.

SAILOR'S WARNING

While degrees are technically divided into minutes and seconds, in most cases sailors now use degrees, minutes, and decimal minutes. GPS's and newer charts reflect this change, but many older charts and guidebooks may still show seconds, so be sure to note that these two coordinates mean the same thing:

24°26.75' N, 81°59.5' W and 24°26'45" N, 81°59'30" W

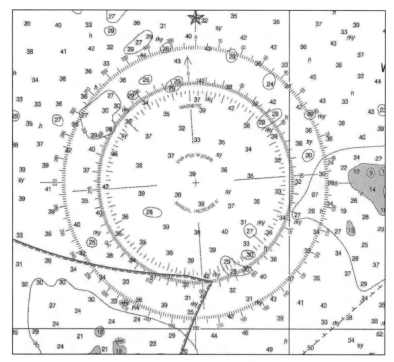

Use the compass rose nearest to the section of chart you are traveling through (most charts will have two or more) and note that true compass direction is printed around the outside, and magnetic compass direction is printed around the inside.
(NOAA)

Dead Reckoning

Paper and compass navigation may seem complex, but in fact it's more like a variation on those grade school math problems: if you have set sail and traveled west from the channel entrance buoy at 3.5 knots, where are you after 2 hours? This particular math problem is called *dead reckoning*. With dead reckoning you start from a known position (such as a buoy) and then by multiplying speed by time, you can sort out the distance you've traveled along a specific course (3.5 × 2 = 7 miles).

The problem with dead reckoning, especially for sailboats, is we don't tend to sail in a perfectly straight line, so dead reckoning isn't always accurate. Add the fact that both current and wind can affect your direction and speed, and you can end up with an increasing amount of uncertainty about your exact location as time goes on.

Fixing Your Position

By taking a compass bearing, you can decrease the amount of uncertainty you have about your position. The idea is to choose two or more objects that you can identify on land and locate on your chart and then to point your handheld compass at the object and make note of the bearing. (It's a good idea to double and triple check your bearing.) Then, by transferring this bearing number using the parallel ruler and the compass rose, you can plot a line through the object.

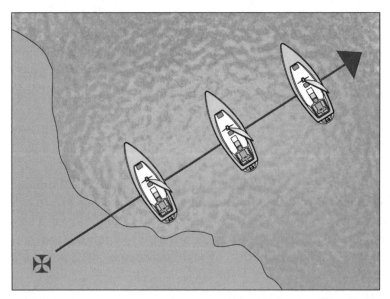

By using your hand-bearing compass and pointing it at a charted object, you can discover a line that your boat is located somewhere along or close to.

If you are only able to get a single fix, this will help you get a clearer idea of where you are, but it's best to use a two- or three-position fix. To do this, you choose objects that are spread roughly 60 to 90° (two objects) or 120° (three objects) apart and take fixes on each object in rapid succession. The result, after you plot each line, should be a point where the lines intersect. Three-position fix likely won't be a perfect intersection, but more of a triangle shape that you are located within.

Follow these steps to take a two- or three-position fix:

- Scan your nautical chart ahead of time. Find and highlight objects you can use for bearings. This will make your plotting faster and easier.

- Choose the first object. Good choices include ranges, lighthouses, church steeples, towers, or recognizable points of land. Keep in mind that sea buoys can be convenient, but they are often moved.

- Line yourself up. Visualize an imaginary line from your eye through the compass to the object. Note the number on the compass.

- Take the info to the chart. Lay the parallel rulers on the compass rose so that an outer edge runs through the compass number and the center point of the magnetic compass rose.

- Transfer the bearing. Carefully walk the ruler (so you don't lose the angle) to the object on the chart and draw a line through the center of the object out to where you think you are.

- Repeat for the second and third bearing. If you do not end up with a triangle (in a three-point fix), try each step again.

BETTER BOATING

Take bearings on objects off your bow or stern first. These bearings will change slowest as you move through the water. Take the compass headings of objects off your beam last. Bearings to these objects change fastest.

The nearer the object you are taking a bearing from, the more accurate your bearing will be.

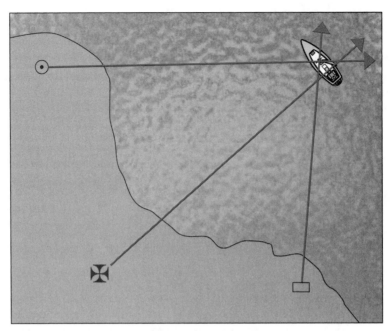

By finding the intersection of three position lines, you can locate a more accurate position of your boat on a chart.

Setting a Course Using Magnetic Bearings Only

Hopefully when you take your bearings and plot your position, you'll find yourself somewhere along the course line you drew before heading out. There are several reasons to plot a course in advance; the most obvious is you'll need to know how far you're going and how long it will take to get there, but you'll also want to plot a course to ensure you avoid dangers.

Keep in mind this is a simplified method of plotting a course using magnetic bearings only. The problem with this method is it requires a current chart with updated variation and a parallel ruler, and if the compass rose is in an awkward place on the chart it can be tricky. The true to magnetic conversion (outlined next) is the method taught by most sailing schools.

To plot a magnetic course, do the following:

- Scan the chart carefully. Look over your planned route, checking for shipping lanes, reefs, areas of current, and other dangers. Also note landmarks you can use for plotting your position as you travel.

- Draw your course line. Use a parallel ruler to draw a line from your departure point to your destination, or to the first turn in your course.

- Determine the course you need to steer. Place one edge of the parallel rulers along the line and walk it to the center of nearest magnetic compass rose to get your compass course. Write this number above that section of the plotted line in degrees magnetic. For example, 165°M.

- Work out the distance. Determine the distance of the line in nautical miles by measuring it with your dividers and then transferring this to the distance scale on the side of the chart. If the line is longer than your dividers open, measure off a distance from the scale first and then walk the dividers along the course line. Write that number under the course line. For example, 9 miles.

- Repeat the procedure until you have lines drawn all the way to your destination. Add up the distances of each line to calculate the distance of your entire journey. Divide this distance by the speed your boat typically travels to estimate how long it will take to arrive at your destination. For example, if you are traveling for 9 miles and your boat travels at 4.5 knots, it will take roughly 2 hours.

SAILOR'S WARNING

Navigation safety means never relying entirely on a single source of information, regardless of how convincing it seems. This means you should always check the depth sounder against the chart, the chart against your eye, or your eye against the navigation markers.

- Double-check everything. Parallel rulers and protractors can easily slip. And even a minor error can throw your course off by several degrees. By measuring your plotted course twice, and getting the same information each time, you'll know you have it right.

Converting True Courses to Magnetic Courses

If you are navigating in a traditional way (without GPS) you are probably going to need to convert a true course to a magnetic course on a regular basis. Most of us use GPS though, so the skill will only come up occasionally. Converting a true course to a magnetic course requires a bit of math. Don't be too worried—it's only a bit of subtraction and addition.

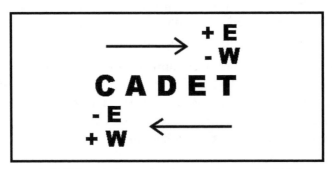

The mnemonic CADET reminds you that Compass (magnetic) Add East variation to get True.
(Evan Gatehouse)

There are two types of variation and deviation: east and west. And you either add or subtract them (keep the CADET mnemonic in mind if you start to get lost).

Here's an example:

If you are trying to work out your position on a chart and your magnetic bearing is 100°M, and the variation is 15°E (noted on your chart) and deviation is 3°E (from your compass deviation card), then true bearing that you need to plot on your chart to find your position = 100°M + 15°E + 3°E = 118°T.

Once you have that concept in mind, you'll also see that if you have west variation you'll need to subtract it. Here's an example of west variation:

If your magnetic bearing is 100°M, and the variation is 20°W (from your chart) and deviation is 2°W (from your compass deviation card), then the true bearing you'll plot on the chart = 100°M – 20°W – 2°W = 78°T.

When you go from a true bearing that you have plotted on a chart to a magnetic compass course that you will use to steer, CADET works backward. You subtract east variation and add west variation. The preceding figure is a good way to visualize this rule. It might be useful to print this on a label and stick one in your logbook or on your protractor or parallel ruler.

The Least You Need to Know

- Having a chart for the area you are sailing in is an essential safety item.
- There are several publications available that can help make piloting your boat safer; *Chart No. 1* and "Notices to Mariners" are two of the more important ones.
- Taking a navigation course will increase your safety on the water.
- Even if you have a GPS and rely on it for navigation, learning and practicing basic navigation skills is still important.
- Navigation safety means never relying entirely on a single source of information, regardless of how convincing it seems.

Marine Electronics

In This Chapter

- Using a GPS
- Understanding your chart plotter
- Using a depth sounder
- Selecting a VHF
- Choosing between other electronic aids

The first time we used a GPS I was amazed. I'd put in the waypoint (the latitude and longitude position of the place we wanted to head toward) for the harbor buoy at our destination, and a few hours of sailing later, I looked through the binoculars and saw the buoy, exactly where the GPS said it would be. Not exactly earth-shattering stuff now, but after years of paper navigating and of cautiously trying to decide, "Which hill is that?" in an endless landscape of matching green hills, it was pretty exciting.

While understanding that basic pen and paper navigation is essential, in truth most sailors are increasingly relying on electronic devices, apps, and gadgets. The GPS, which revolutionized navigation when it became available in the mid 1990s, is arguably one of the most important. But chart plotters, AIS (Automatic Identification System), radar, VHF radios, and depth sounders all offer important information (and extra screens) for sailors to utilize.

The great thing about all these electronics is it means getting lost is difficult. The problem is it's possible to become over reliant on them and make dangerous errors. If you've ever followed your car's GPS the wrong way down a one-way street, you'll know what I mean. The key to using marine electronics is to operate them with an awareness of their limitations. And always make sure that what the screen tells you matches up with the reality of the situation.

Tips for Using Your GPS

Recall the three-point fix we covered in Chapter 9? Well, visualize that idea again for a moment, because a GPS does a sort of high-tech version. Basically it works like this: between 24 and 32 satellites orbit the earth, and your receiver gets signals from several of them. And by determining the time it took those signals to arrive, a calculation is made which pinpoints your three-dimensional location in latitude, longitude, and altitude.

As a boater, you can then take those numbers (altitude is probably not required) and plot them on your chart to discover exactly where you are.

Your GPS will have a variety of screen views which give a range of different information to help with navigation.
(Garmin International)

While a GPS can tell you where you are, it can also tell you where you're going. By keying in waypoints, you can obtain information from your GPS that includes:

- The course you need to steer

- The distance and time to your next waypoint, or to your destination

- The distance you have traveled so far

- The speed you are traveling over the ground (as opposed to your knotmeter, which tells you how quickly you are moving through the water)

If navigating with a GPS sounds straightforward, that's because it is. Keep in mind, though, that GPSs come with a variety of functions and features (from anchor alarms to man overboard buttons), so reading the instruction book or watching the tutorial video is essential. Many navigation schools also offer additional training for using a GPS.

NAUTICAL KNOWLEDGE

GPS was developed as a military navigation system, and initially civilians received a degraded signal that wasn't particularly accurate. "Selective Availability" was turned off in 2000 after the U.S. government realized that an accurate GPS system would be useful in everyday applications. The system has continued to receive upgrades and becomes more and more accurate as time goes on.

When using a GPS, keep the following tips in mind:

- Check and double check your waypoints when you are entering them into the GPS.

- If using waypoints from another source (e.g., a friend gives you a waypoint for a great anchorage, or you're using a waypoint list from a guidebook), first plot the numbers on your chart to make sure they make sense. Errors can be common.

- Continue to keep track of visual landmarks; don't just rely on the GPS. This strategy ensures that if your GPS malfunctions (or you did make an error), you don't run into trouble, or land.

- Always plot the entire route on a chart before you enter your destination waypoints into the GPS and hit the "go to" button. You don't want to discover the hard way that there was a reef in the way.

- Never make your waypoint a solid object such as a buoy, lighthouse, or breakwater. GPSs can be very accurate and boaters have been known to run right into their waypoint.

- Keep track of your progress and plot your position on your chart at regular intervals. To do this you would use the GPS numbers to plot your position and then compare it against what you see outside. This way, if your GPS fails, you'll have an accurate idea of where you are.

Navigating consists of three things:

- Knowing where you are
- Knowing where you are going
- Knowing exactly what hazards exist between your departure point and your destination

Tips for Using a Chart Plotter

Through the ages, sailors have been in search of new technology to make navigation safer and more accurate. The GPS was one step, but considering the scope of information the GPS provides (not to mention the information your depth sounder, radar, and AIS might be offering to the equation), a human navigator working on a paper chart can't always cope with all the data that's coming in. A simple solution is to use a chart plotter to integrate and display all that information on an electronic chart.

The chart plotter's main strength is it updates your position continuously and lets you plan routes without the risk of introducing errors (such as plotting the waypoint 47°35.61'N when you meant to use 47°36.51'N). Plotters do have their drawbacks. The small screen can make noticing hazards on longer routes more difficult, a detail that was highlighted in a well-publicized Southern California tragedy when a sailboat ran into an island while traveling to Mexico.

A chart plotter combines GPS technology with electronic charts to give you a live-action display showing your progress through the water.
(Garmin International)

Complex integrated chart plotting systems that interface with all your other electronics and take into account tidal stream, wind speed, and wind direction, and that give simple steering instructions, are expensive, and don't make much sense on a small boat. But basic plotters, which allow you to mark waypoints and plan routes, are growing increasingly popular.

BETTER BOATING

Smart phones and tablets can make great backup chart plotters (or a primary one if your main navigation is done the traditional way). Phones and tablets with apps including iNavX and plan2Nav or software such as Navionics can't do everything a high-tech integrated system can do (such as engaging the autopilot, overlaying the radar display with the chart display, going split-screen with the depth sounder, or integrating with AIS), but they can provide basic chart plotting technology at a reasonable price—especially if you already own the device. See appendix A for more app options.

If do you use a chart plotter for navigation, keep in mind that these offer useful extra features (including pictures, notes, and satellite overviews) but may not tell the whole navigational story. Especially if you are using charts for other countries, you'll want to keep the following in mind:

- GPS positions can be bang on, or off by several yards, depending on the receiver type and the conditions—which will affect your chart plotter. You may find yourself off course or even off the chart.

- While your GPS might pinpoint your position to within a few feet, chances are the chart plotter won't. In some cases you may be using charts based on surveys conducted by someone with a lead line on a sailboat. At times our charting software has shown us on shore when we were clearly in a channel (thankfully we haven't had this scenario go the other way round).

- Occasionally, important details (such as reefs) are completely missed (on international charts) or only shown at a particular level of zoom on the screen, although the information is visible on a paper chart. This can be a serious problem when you are planning a route and the screen doesn't show a known hazard that's in your way.

Getting the Most Out of Your Depth Sounder

The process of figuring out how deep the water is and what's on the bottom has come a very long way since the time when sailors heaved lead lines over the side to measure the depth and test the bottom. With the advent of SONAR (SOund NAvigation and Ranging) technology, we started to get a picture of what the bottom looked like. And as fish finders improve, so does the quality of information we receive.

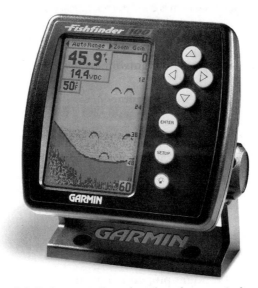

Depth-sounding fish finders can tell you how deep the water is, how rapidly the depth is changing and give you an idea what the bottom material is.
(Garmin International)

Modern fish finders can help you find the fish (if that's what you're looking for), but as sailors we're typically more interested in knowing the depth (and how rapidly it might be changing), the water temperature, and discovering what the bottom is made up of. Here are some tips for using your depth sounder:

• Keep in mind that the depth of the water is measured from the location of the transducer (the part of the depth sounder that is found somewhere on the hull), not the screen where the image is displayed. For example, if the transducer is attached to the hull 2 feet below the water line and your boat draws (has a depth of) 5 feet, this means you would go aground when the depth sounder reads 3 feet. Sailing-oriented depth sounders do allow you to input your keel depth, so the instrument can calculate the true water depth.

- Despite the way the readout may look, depth sounders tell you what's directly below you—they do not look ahead or to either side and can't, without your help, keep you off a shoal.

- Shallow water alarms are useful while anchoring or while traveling through channels with poorly marked sides. The deep water alarm can also be useful in certain situations.

- Deducing the bottom's composition typically takes a bit of practice. A hard bottom such as clay or sand shows up as a thin dark line. A softer mud bottom or a bottom covered with seaweed will produce a wide, sometimes wavering line. A bottom covered with rocks or coral will "look" rocky and uneven, while a wreck will appear irregular and jagged.

- Sometimes you'll see two bottoms. This can happen when the bottom is soft and there is a hard layer below it, or if the sensitivity to the depth sounder is turned up too high.

Always try to confirm that the bottom you see on your depth sounder corresponds with what the nautical chart says is down there. If you look at a chart, you'll see specific abbreviations for the nature of the sea bed:

> S = Sand
>
> M = Mud
>
> Cy = Clay
>
> G = Gravel
>
> P = Pebbles
>
> R; rky = Rocky
>
> Co = Coral
>
> S/M = Sand over Mud
>
> Wd = Weed (including kelp)

These basic abbreviations may be qualified by extra details, including images of weed or rocks or additional abbreviations:

> f = Fine (for sand)
>
> m = Medium (sand)
>
> c = Coarse (sand)
>
> bk = Broken
>
> sy = Sticky
>
> so = Soft
>
> sf = Stiff

If in doubt, check section J, "the nature of the seabed," in *Chart No. 1* (see App A for more information on this publication).

VHF Radios

Even if you opt for no other electronics, a VHF (very high frequency) radio is an essential piece of equipment. VHFs come in two forms: handheld (used as backup, or on a very small boat) or fixed mount. Most boats opt for a fixed mount version, but with today's small waterproof handheld VHF radios, it's possible (not to mention wise and affordable) to carry a VHF radio even while sailing a small dinghy.

VHF radios offer only short-range line-of-sight communications (5–30 miles), but they're useful for talking with other boats in your area, calling a lock or bridge operator, or seeking help in emergency situations. There's more to using a radio than just buying it and twisting the knobs, though. You have to know how to make clear and accurate communication.

First of all, unlike a phone, a radio won't let you talk and listen at the same time. Because radios operate on only one frequency, your voice goes out and the reply comes back in on the same channel. To make this work, you must press a button, talk, release the button, and then listen for the reply.

Most people leave their radios on and switched to Channel 16 when underway. This is known as the distress frequency. Its purpose is to provide an open channel for all parties to listen in and see if anyone is in need of help. You can also use 16 as a "hailing channel" to reach another boat.

Handheld radios are a great option for small dinghies, but if you are able to install one, a fixed mount radio has a greater range.

(Evan Gatehouse)

You may wonder whether you need a license to operate a VHF radio. VHF radio operator licenses are not required in the United States, unless you're visiting other countries. Canada and most other countries do require them. Canada also requires a station license (for the boat) if travelling internationally.

To make a radio call, follow these steps:

- Select the channel you will be calling from. If you are calling the Coast Guard or another vessel, this will be channel 16. Bridges, locks, marinas, gas docks, etc. are normally hailed on different channels in different regions, so check your local cruising guide.

- Make sure the power is on and the volume is up. Listen for other traffic on the channel before making your call. If all you hear is static, rotate the squelch knob until the static just stops.

- Press the button and call your party three times, Saying your name only once. For example, "Garden Cove Marina, Garden Cove Marina, Garden Cove Marina, this is the sailing vessel *Charm*."

- After making contact, change channels if required. In order to keep 16 free for emergencies, you'll need to choose another channel (68, 69, 71, 72, and 78A are noncommercial working channels in the United States).

- After switching channels, both you and the person you hailed will listen to see if the channel is clear. If you hear a conversation, you both switch back to 16, connect with each other again, and choose a new channel.

- Remember that the conversations on a VHF can be heard by anyone listening to the channel you're on, so don't expect privacy.

Watch the lingo. Nothing says rookie like talking on the VHF as though it's a CB radio. Use the following:

- *Roger:* This means you understood what was said.

- *Affirmative:* Means yes. "Uh-huh," "sure," "yup," etc. can be hard to hear and understand.

- *Negative:* Means no.

- *Over:* Said at the end of a transmission, it means you've finished your statement.

- *Out:* Means you've finished the call and are returning to the hailing channel.

When details (such as your name or your boat's name) are especially important, you may be asked to spell things phonetically to avoid confusion. Use the following chart for spelling phonetically:

The International Phonetic Alphabet

Letter	Phonetic Letter
A	Alpha
B	Bravo
C	Charlie
D	Delta
E	Echo
F	Foxtrot
G	Golf
H	Hotel

Letter	Phonetic Letter
I	India
J	Juliet
K	Kilo
L	Lima
M	Mike
N	November
O	Oscar
P	Papa
Q	Quebec
R	Romeo
S	Sierra
T	Tango
U	Uniform
V	Victor
W	Whiskey
X	X-ray
Y	Yankee
Z	Zulu

Many boat owners opt to keep a copy of their boat name spelled phonetically in a handy location in case it's needed.

SAILOR'S WARNING

When you hear a distress call, give the Coast Guard a chance to respond. If they respond, just listen and do not press your mike button. If they don't answer after 2 minutes, you'll need to answer the call yourself. Do this by getting the details of the emergency and then either relay the information to the authorities (along with your own position) or provide whatever assistance you're able to safely offer.

Like most electronics, VHFs come in very simple models or ones with a whole range of features including:

- *Digital Selective Calling* (DSC) capability: Part of the *Global Maritime Distress Safety System (GMDSS)*, DSC also has several nonemergency features, including the ability to privately call another boat or send and receive GPS positions.

> **DEFINITION**
>
> The **Global Maritime Distress Safety System (GMDSS)** is an internationally developed set of safety procedures and communication practices to make it easier to rescue vessels in distress.

- *GPS or AIS combos:* Rather than having multiple separate units and having to tie everything together, these are built into the radio.

- *Secondary Stations:* This is a second microphone in a convenient location so, for example, you can be on the wheel and on the radio at the same time.

- *Foghorn functions:* You can have your radio broadcast sound signals for operating in reduced visibility. The settings include under way, stopped, sailing, aground, etc.

- *Weather Alerts:* Most radios can notify you when they detect a special weather warning signal from NOAA and will inform you about thunderstorms or other extreme weather. Specific Area Message Encoding (S.A.M.E.) is available on some radios and ensures you only get localized warnings.

Gizmos and Gadgets or Safety Essentials?

Sailing can be as simple (just you and the wind) or as technologically advanced (you, the wind, and six different readouts) as you like. Some of the electronic options have been around for years—pretty much everyone knows about radar and VHF radios, for example—while other options, such as AIS and Spot, are new enough that it's still open to debate whether they can be considered essential or not.

Part of deciding what's right for you is based on the size of your boat, where you're going to be sailing (Does it get foggy or are sudden thunderstorms a likelihood? Is the region lightly or heavily populated? Do you need to cross shipping lanes?), who you're sailing with (short-handed sailors will often opt for extra electronics as a second or third set of eyes), and how much you want to spend.

But the big factor is often comfort. Some people simply prefer to have the most modern safety and navigation equipment, while others don't.

Radar

Radar, or RAdio Detection And Ranging, is a technology that uses electromagnetic waves to identify moving or fixed objects, including ships, sea buoys, approaching storms, or land. It's especially useful at night or in reduced visibility (such as in the fog or during a downpour), or when entering a crowded anchorage and trying to find a "hole" to fit into. But even during the day it's sometimes very helpful to know that you are 1.4 miles off a dangerous point, or positioned exactly in the center of a narrow channel.

Learning to interpret what's on your radar screen takes practice. One good technique is to practice with your radar during good visibility, when you can compare what is happening both on screen and in reality.

AIS

The Automated Identity System was developed to help prevent collisions between commercial shipping vessels, but sailors and other recreational boaters are finding that the system works well for us, too. The simplest AIS device is a "receive-only device." Included as part of AIS-equipped VHF radios or chart plotters, the receiver collects data from ships with transponders. The information includes ship name, its direction and speed of travel, and the closest distance the ship will get to you.

What this means is if you are sailing along and notice that a ship looks like it is on a collision course, rather than using your hand-bearing compass to see if you are going to cross paths, you simply look at the display on your AIS receiver. If the information indicates the ship will get too close, you can call the ship directly, by name even, and make a plan to avoid collision.

Not all vessels are AIS equipped. Only commercial ships over 65 feet and tugs over 26 feet and over 600 HP are required to have transponders. Some larger recreational vessels will have transponders, but remember: although you can see them on screen, they don't have the same data for you.

SPOT

New satellite messaging devices such as the SPOT Messenger are becoming increasingly popular with recreational sailors. Used by boaters who are not traveling far enough to require service of an EPIRB (Emergency Position Indicating Radio Beacon), these gadgets can be a cool tracking and communication device. For example, SPOT's tracking feature sends your GPS location to a Google Map every 10 minutes, so friends and family at home can track your progress and know when to meet you at the dock.

A SPOT device lets your family at home track your sailing progress.
(The SPOT Satellite GPS Messenger ™, by SPOT, LLC, a wholly owned subsidiary of
Globalstar, Inc. For more information, please visit www.findmespot.com.)

Keep in mind if you do get a personal messenger device that, unlike a 406 EPIRB
or a Personal Locator Beacon (PLB), these systems are not part of the GMDSS, and
your distress signal is first routed through a private monitoring service before being
directed to search-and-rescue agencies such as the U.S. Coast Guard.

Autopilot

An autopilot is pretty much what it sounds like—a device that hooks up to the tiller
or wheel then steers the course that you set for as long as you want. Uncommon
on boats under 25 feet or so, various versions are pretty common on larger boats.
Autopilots (tiller pilots if you have a tiller) let you safely navigate, grab lunch, adjust
sails, or simply lounge in the cockpit while the boat holds a steady course.

Unless you have a high-tech version, they won't adjust to wind shifts and can't sail out
of the way of danger unless you tell them to.

The Least You Need to Know

- GPS technology makes navigation much simpler than using traditional methods.

- Chart plotters can improve the ease of navigation, but consulting paper charts is still considered important.

- Fish finding depth sounders don't just give you the water depth, they can also indicate the material on the sea bottom.

- Of the wide variety of electronics that can provide additional information to make navigation safer and more accurate, the VHF radio is probably one of the most essential.

- Relying just on electronics to keep you out of trouble isn't a safe practice; you need to always be aware of what's happening in real life.

Rules of the (Watery) Road

In This Chapter

- Reading the buoys (and other signs)
- Determining who has right of way
- Using whistles and horns to signal your plans
- Using and understanding nighttime navigation lights

Right this moment I'm looking out over our small but busy harbor. There's a kayak group out exploring; three personal watercraft are zipping around; two small powerboats have people fishing from them and several more are just out for a ride; there's a few day sailors enjoying a light breeze; and a couple of larger sailboats are raising their sails. Aside from the pleasure boats, there are two small harbor ferries making regular runs, a tug with a barge under tow, and a few commercial tour boats out on harbor tours.

Despite the fact there are no stop signs or traffic lights, on-ramps or lane dividers, every boat in the harbor seems to know what to do. The tug just blew its horn twice and then altered course to port. A sailboat steered out of the way of the group of kayakers. And when a powerboat and a personal watercraft came toward each other head on, they both steered to miss one another.

Between rules of the road, navigational signals, and commonsense, everyone seems to be enjoying the water. The key, though, is to know these rules before you join all the boats on a busy harbor. You need to know what that horn blast meant and which way to alter course (if at all). You need to know what your boat is expected to do in a head-on situation and how to react if someone overtakes you.

Buoys and Markers

Buoys and markers can be thought of as the nautical equivalent of street signs. While they can seem a bit confusing at first, keep in mind that they really have one main purpose: to keep you from running aground. Because running aground is inconvenient at best, and dangerous or damaging at worst, over time a standardized system of markers and buoys was developed to keep you in the deep water and away from above- or underwater dangers.

Q Buoys and Beacons

e		Mid-channel buoy (red and white vertical stripe)	RW	
f		Starboard-hand buoy (entering from seaward - US waters)	R "2"	
g		Port-hand buoy (entering from seaward - US waters)	G "1" "1"	
h		Bifurcation, Junction, Isolated danger, Wreck and Obstruction buoys	BR RG GR G	
i		Fish trap (area) buoy	Y	
j		Anchorage buoy (marks limits)	Y	
l		Triangular shaped beacons	▲ R △ RG Bn	
		Square shaped beacons	■ G □ GR □ W □ B Bn Bn Bn	
		Beacon, color unknown	□ Bn	
m		Mooring buoy with telegraphic communications	Tel Tel	
n		Mooring buoy with telephonic communications	T T	
o		Lighted beacon		! Bn
q		Security barrier	Security Barrier	
r		Scientific mooring buoy		
s		FLOAT		
t		White and Blue buoy		WBU

Charts use specific symbols to represent the buoys you'll see on the water.
(NOAA)

It might surprise you, but the majority of these buoys and markers are different than street signs in they don't have instructions or information printed on them. In a marine environment where distance, fog, rain, or low light could make words difficult to see and understand, they use color and shape to provide information. Some buoys and markers also use solar-powered lights to help with nighttime navigation.

The system is pretty straightforward, (though keep in mind it isn't the same in every country), but by using (and understanding) a system of predictable buoys, you'll know where to go.

BETTER BOATING

Good binoculars make identifying marks and buoys much easier. A set of 7×50 binoculars tends to be the standard with boaters. This is because a magnification power of seven makes it easier to find an object and keep it in view, and the 50mm lenses are large enough to be useful in low light conditions and provide a wide field of view. Using binoculars of a higher magnification or smaller lens can make sighting and holding objects difficult, especially on a moving boat. Look for binoculars that have a water-resistant or waterproof design to avoid moisture-related damage. Some also come with a built-in compass or image stabilization.

Lateral Buoys and Marks

Lateral buoys are used to identify the borders of channels. When traveling upstream, which refers to the direction the tide floods, you'll notice that port-hand (green) buoys are kept on the port side of your boat and the starboard-hand (red) buoys are kept to starboard. The reverse of this is true when you head downstream. A favorite way to remember which buoy goes where is to keep in mind the 3Rs: red, right, returning. This means keep the **red** buoys on your **right** side when **returning** into a harbor (or heading up-river, or sailing toward a shoreline).

NAUTICAL KNOWLEDGE

The International Association of Marine Aids to Navigation and Lighthouse Authorities (IALA) has two worldwide regions which use two different systems of buoys and markers (a huge improvement on the 30+ systems in use before 1976). The United States and Canada (as well as the rest of North and South America, Japan, South Korea, and the Philippines) are in region B. IALA region A covers most of the rest of the world and uses a system which is essentially IALA B in reverse (or we use IALA A in reverse …). So in IALA A, rather than red, right, returning it would be green, right, returning.

Starboard-hand lateral marks are red with a triangle-shaped cone on top. Keep them to the right when entering a harbor.

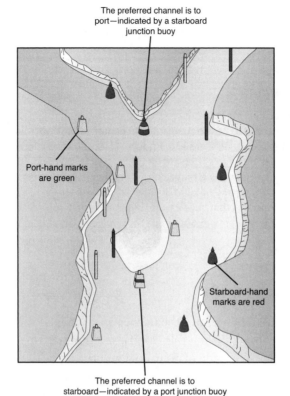

The preferred channel is to
port—indicated by a starboard
junction buoy

Port-hand marks
are green

Starboard-hand
marks are red

The preferred channel is to
starboard—indicated by a port junction buoy

*By paying attention to the channel markers, it's possible
to safely navigate narrow channels.*

Lateral buoys mark out channels and show you where to steer to keep your boat in safe water. Always compare the buoys on hand with your chart, especially after stormy weather, which can cause them to shift around. Marks are also moved when sandbars shift. Important or well-used channels will often have lit buoys (often operated by solar-powered batteries). The light sequences (the pattern of flashes the light displays) will vary from location to location, but those unique flashes can help you identify a marker.

There are two types of lateral buoys:

- *Port-hand buoys:* Green in color, port-hand buoys also have a cylinder-shaped top mark. When they have a light it will be green flashing (see your chart for the specific pattern) and it may be identified by letters and odd numbers. These buoys mark the left-hand side of a channel (when facing upstream). When heading into harbor, keep the green buoys on your port side even if no red buoys are evident.

• *Starboard-hand buoys:* Red in color, starboard-hand buoys have a triangle-shaped red cone pointing upward. Lights will be quick-flashing red (see your chart for the specific pattern), and the buoy be may marked with letters and even numbers. These buoys mark the right-hand side of a channel (when facing upstream). When heading into harbor, keep the red buoys on the starboard side of your boat and travel between the green and red buoys if both are visible.

> **SAILOR'S WARNING**
>
> Never travel too close to a buoy or marker or attempt to tie up to one. In some cases they are in shallow water and are attached directly to the seabed (so you run the risk of running aground). In other cases they may be anchored to the bottom, and you run the risk of getting caught in their mooring cables.

Junction (Bifurcation) Buoys and Marks

Just as it sounds, these red/green buoys indicate a junction in the channel. Depending on the markings, they will show where the preferred and secondary channels are. Always study the chart in advance so you know which channel you want to take.

There are two types of junction (bifurcation) buoys:

• *Port junction (bifurcation) buoys:* Green with a red midsection, you can travel on either side of this marker but to enter the preferred channel, keep a port junction buoy on your port side when returning to port.

• *Starboard junction (bifurcation) buoys:* Red with a green middle; to keep to the main channel, keep this buoy on your starboard side when returning to port.

> **BETTER BOATING**
>
> While junction buoys can look tricky, here's a tip: the top band indicates the preferred channel. So if you want to stay in the main channel and the top color is red, read the junction buoy as a solid red buoy and leave it to starboard if you are returning to harbor.

Fairway and Isolated Danger Buoys and Marks

The lateral buoy system also includes fairway buoys and isolated danger buoys, which are pretty much as they sound. Fairway buoys mark the center of a large channel, while isolated danger buoys mark small specific hazards.

- *Fairway buoys:* Half red, half white (divided vertically), these buoys indicate that while there is safe water on all sides, it should typically be kept to port.

These red and white buoys are often found in deeper water and are mostly useful to large ships (and sea lions).
(Evan Gatehouse)

- *Isolated danger buoys:* Painted black with a horizontal red stripe midway up, these buoys are used to mark a hazard like a rock, shoal, or a wreck. They are located directly on or above the danger. To be safe, check your chart for information and give these buoys a wide berth.

Cardinal Buoys and Marks

Cardinal buoys are used less frequently in IALA B than they are in IALA A, but if you do encounter them, it's good to know what they mean:

- *North cardinal buoy:* Topped with two stacked black cones, both pointing up (imagine a compass needle pointing north), the body is black on the top and yellow on the bottom. This buoy indicates that the safest water lies to the north. Any light will be flashing white; see your chart for the pattern.

North cardinal mark: pass to the north.
Light will be continuous, quick-flashing white.

East cardinal mark: pass to the east.
Light will be white, flashing in groups of three very quick flashes.

South cardinal mark: pass to the south.
Light will be white, flashing in groups of six very quick flashes.

West cardinal mark: pass to the west.
Light will be white, flashing in groups of nine very quick flashes.

Cardinal marks are used to show where the deep-water side of a hazard is located.

- *South cardinal buoy:* The top half is yellow and the bottom half is black. The top mark is two black cones pointing down (imagine a compass needle pointing south). If it is equipped with a light, this will be white (see your chart for the flash pattern). This buoy indicates the safe water lies to the south.

- *East cardinal buoy:* These are black with one broad horizontal yellow band around the middle. The top mark has two black cones; the top one points up, the bottom points down. If it has a light, it will be flashing white with a specific pattern found on your chart. This buoy indicates that the safest water lies to the east.

- *West cardinal buoy:* These are yellow with one broad horizontal black band around the middle. The top mark has two black cones that point together; imagine a wasp-waisted woman. If it has a light it will be flashing white with a specific pattern found on your chart. This buoy signifies that the safest water lies to the west.

Additional Buoys and Marks

Additional buoys include yellow buoys and daybeacons:

- *Yellow buoys:* Yellow means caution on land and on the water. They are often used to indicate pipes, temporary dredge lines, traffic schemes, or a new danger. Check your chart (or "Notice to Mariners" in the case of a new buoy) if you see a yellow buoy, to learn its significance. If in doubt: stay away.

BETTER BOATING

If you are on the Intracoastal Waterway (ICW) on the U.S. East Coast, aids to navigation will be the normal red and green colors and shapes, but they will also have some portion marked with yellow to identify them as being part of the waterway.

- *Daybeacons:* In shallow water buoys don't make sense, so daymarks are used instead. Other than the fact they are signs on posts rather than floating buoys, these markers use the same colors, shapes, lights, and numbers as buoys.

Lights and Their Sequences

Lights on buoys, beacons, and lighthouses have a wide variety of flash patterns so you can sort out what you're seeing. For example, if two red-lighted buoys were next to each other and had the same flash pattern, you wouldn't be able to tell which you should be using. The following are some of the common flash patterns you'll run into:

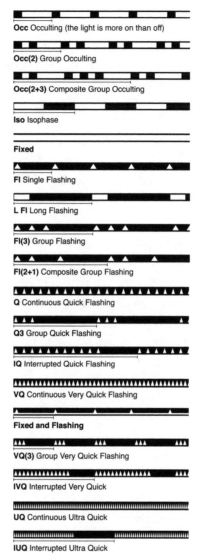

Occ Occulting (the light is more on than off)

Occ(2) Group Occulting

Occ(2+3) Composite Group Occulting

Iso Isophase

Fixed

Fl Single Flashing

L Fl Long Flashing

Fl(3) Group Flashing

Fl(2+1) Composite Group Flashing

Q Continuous Quick Flashing

Q3 Group Quick Flashing

IQ Interrupted Quick Flashing

VQ Continuous Very Quick Flashing

Fixed and Flashing

VQ(3) Group Very Quick Flashing

IVQ Interrupted Very Quick

UQ Continuous Ultra Quick

IUQ Interrupted Ultra Quick

*Check your chart for the exact sequence of the lights you are looking for or consult
the correct volume of the U.S. Coast Guard's Light List:
navcen.uscg.gov/?pageName=lightLists*

Rules of the Road

Let me say, right off the bat, when talking about boats, the term *right of way* isn't really accurate. We all use it, people think they know what it means, but we'll focus on the correct terms right from the start. When two vessels are close enough to each other that the possibility of a collision exists, one vessel is always designated by the rules as the stand-on vessel and the other is the give-way vessel.

What does this mean in a practical (and legal) sense? In most cases it means the stand-on vessel should maintain its course and speed, while the give-way vessel needs to alter its course and/or speed early enough to avoid the collision in a large obvious maneuver. This is the scenario that leads people to think that the stand-on vessel has right of way.

But there's another rule: if it's clear the give-way vessel isn't, well, giving way, then the stand-on vessel must make an obvious move to avoid the collision. So when you look at it this way, no one has the right of way and everyone is responsible to avoid a crash.

Just like on land, where traffic rules cover everyone from pedestrians to 18 wheelers, there are rules that govern vessels on the water. Called Collision Regulations, or Col Regs, this very long, very detailed set of regulations outlines pretty much every possible scenario in language like this: "A vessel required not to impede the passage or safe passage of another vessel is not relieved of this obligation if approaching the other vessel so as to involve risk of collision and shall, when taking action, have full regard to the action which may be required by the rules of this part."

So, while you may find it handy to have a copy of the *Col Regs* on hand (you can find it online at the U.S. Coast Guard's Navigation center: navcen.uscg.gov/?pageName=navRulesContent), most people find it easier to remember the rules that apply to them.

Most rules are pretty straightforward:

- You must always have a proper lookout paying attention.

- You must travel at a safe speed that allows you to avoid collisions.

- You must do all you can to avoid collisions.

- In a narrow channel you keep to starboard.

- In restricted conditions, smaller vessels must not impede the bigger, less maneuverable ones. (Think of this one as might is right.)

- When you are crossing a big ship traffic channel (marked by a magenta rectangle on your chart), you must do it as close to a right angle if possible.

Types of Vessels

The way we apply the rules of the road often comes down to the type of vessel you encounter. To make it easier to visualize, vessels are put in a hierarchy. The top vessel (listed first in the following list) is least able to maneuver, so it is the stand-on vessel and every other vessel must keep out of its way. The bottom vessel—the power-driven vessel—listed last on the following list), must give way to every other vessel:

- *Vessels not under command:* A vessel that for some exceptional circumstance is unable to maneuver out of the way of other vessels. Damaged steering or an unconscious operator would fit; going down below to use the head doesn't.

- *Vessels restricted in their ability to maneuver:* If a ship is too large or doing something (dredging, towing a barge) that affects its ability to maneuver.

- *Vessels constrained by draft:* This is a ship that can't maneuver without the risk of running aground.

- *Fishing vessels engaged in fishing:* This means boats where the fishing nets restrict maneuverability; so commercial boats with nets out, not a runabout fishing in the harbor.

- *Sailing vessels:* This is you; but only if the sails are up and your engine is off.

- *Power-driven vessels:* Any vessel propelled by machinery, i.e., an engine. A sailboat is considered a powerboat anytime the engine is on, even if your sails are up.

A power-driven vessel must give way to four types of vessels:

- A vessel not under command

- A vessel restricted in her ability to maneuver

- A vessel engaged in fishing

- A sailing vessel

A sailing vessel must give way to three types of vessels:

- A vessel not under command

- A vessel restricted in her ability to maneuver

- A vessel engaged in fishing

Crossing Situations

Most of the time, though, you're not going to be worried about giving way to a dredge or a fishing boat. Instead you're going to be pondering what to do when you and another sailboat or powerboat are headed right at each other.

When two sailboats are headed toward each other, the rules are:

- Port gives way to starboard. When each sailboat has wind on a different side and you are sailing on different tack, the vessel on a port tack must give way, while the starboard tack boat must hold her course.

- Windward gives way to leeward. When both boats are on the same tack and have the wind on the same side, the windward vessel gives way to the leeward one.

- Port gives way. If you are on a port tack and can't tell what tack the other boat is on, you must give way.

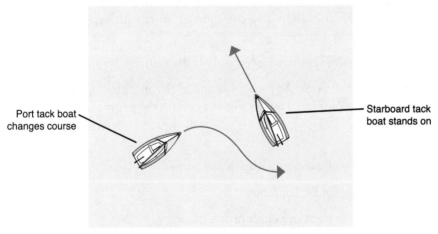

Sailing boats on opposite tacks.

With two boats under power, there are slightly different rules:

- When two powerboats are crossing, "the vessel on the right has right of way." In other words, if you are approaching the port side of a boat, you must give way. This is easier to visualize at night; if you see a red light crossing right-to-left in front of you, you'll need to alter course.

- Typically the give-way vessel will make a large, early course change to starboard. This is so that you avoid crossing ahead of the other vessel. If a starboard course change isn't possible (because of other ships or hazards), you'll want to slow down enough that the other boat can see what you have done.

- Two boats meeting head-on or converging both alter course to starboard so that they pass on the port side of the other.

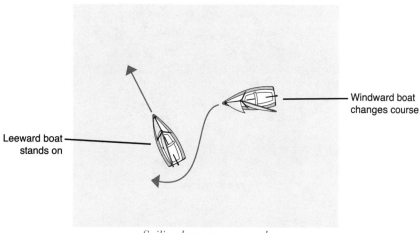

Leeward boat stands on

Windward boat changes course

Sailing boats on same tack.

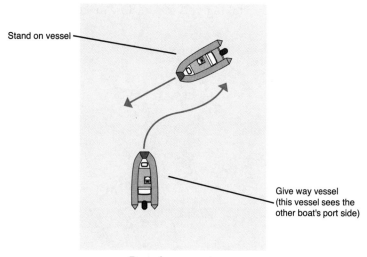

Stand on vessel

Give way vessel (this vessel sees the other boat's port side)

Powerboats crossing.

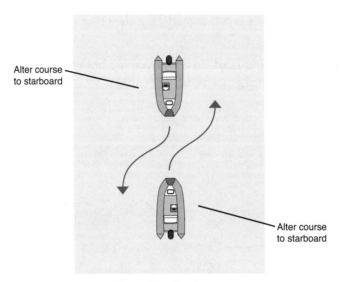

Powerboats head-on.

The final major rule is for overtaking. If you find yourself coming up on another boat, it's your duty to stay clear of them; it's not their job to move out of your way. Keep in mind, though, that if you are traveling up a narrow channel and a large unwieldy looking boat is overtaking you, it probably makes good sense to move.

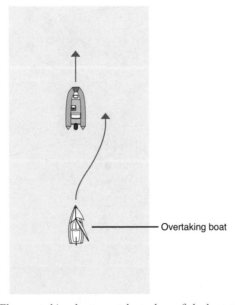

The overtaking rule: The overtaking boat must keep clear of the boat ahead, even if it's a sailboat sailing past a powerboat.

Sound Signals

Though sound signals are uncommon for sailboats and other recreational vessels to use, larger commercial ships will often use horn blasts to let you know what they are up to. Blasts are either short, about 1 second in duration, or long, about 3 seconds.

Here's what the most commonly used signals mean:

- One short blast: The ship is letting you know it's altering course to starboard.
- Two short blasts: The ship is altering course to port.
- Three short blasts: The ship is going into reverse.
- Five short blasts: The ship is signaling danger; or, the ship is confused about what another vessel is doing and is worried about a collision.
- One long blast: The vessel has restricted visibility; it might be approaching a blind bend in the river.

SAILOR'S WARNING

If you hear five short blasts, pay attention. Sort out where the sound has come from as soon as possible; a ship may be trying to tell you that they are concerned by how close you are, or are unsure about the course you are following. In this situation, make your intentions very obvious and begin to move away from the large vessel as quickly as possible.

Navigation Lights

While buoys, beacons, lighthouses, and ranges all will have their unique signature light sequences, boats are a little more predictable. Every type of boat will show a specific combination of red, green, and white lights, so after dark you can tell if you're looking at a boat under sail, a vessel under tow, a powerboat under 65 feet, or a really large freighter.

The Col Regs specify the exact type of lights every boat needs to display from dusk to dawn. Be aware that, as a sailboat, your light configuration will change whenever you turn on the engine.

Basic Navigation Lights

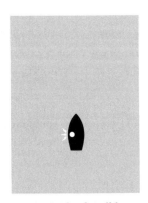

White Light: Small boats under 23 feet sailing or rowing must carry a white light. (A flashlight will work.)

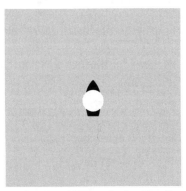

All-around White Light: Small boats under 23 feet motoring capable of under 7 knots must show an all-around white light.

Separate Lights: Sailboats over 65 feet have to use separate sidelights and a sternlight.

Masthead Tricolor: Sailboats under 65 feet that are under sail may show a masthead tricolor light (but when under power the sailboat still has to show powerboat lights).

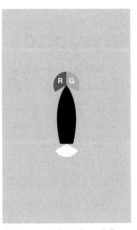

Stern and Combined Bow Sidelights: Sailboats over 23 feet show red and green sidelights and a sternlight.

Steaming Lights

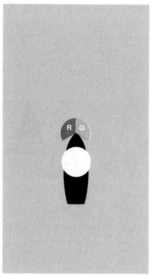

Combined Stern/Masthead Light: Powerboat under 65 feet may combine the stern and masthead lights. Sidelights can be separate or combined in a single bow-mounted light.

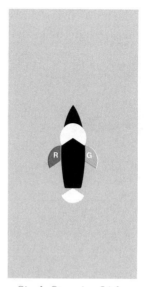

Single Steaming Light: Powerboats less than 160 feet have to show a masthead steaming light, sidelights, and a sternlight.

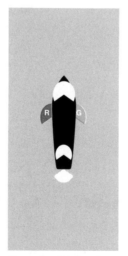

Two Steaming Lights: Large power vessels over 160 feet show two steaming lights. The aft one is higher than the forward one, which helps you judge the direction of the vessel.

Recognizing Navigation Lights

In the following, red navigation lights are indicated in dark blue, green navigation lights are light blue, and white lights are white.

Powerboat less than 65 feet: A powerboat has combined sidelights at the bow and a single masthead light.

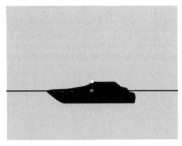

Powerboat greater than 65 feet: A powerboat over 65 feet has separate sidelights. If it was over 160 feet, it would need two masthead lights.

Sailing Vessel less than 65 feet: Under 65 feet, a masthead tricolor light can be used, combining sidelights and sternlights.

Sailing Vessel Optional: Over 65 feet, separate side lights and stern lights are used. Large sailboats may show optional all-around red over green lights.

Hovercraft: Shows the same lights as a powerboat plus an all-around flashing yellow light.

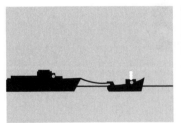

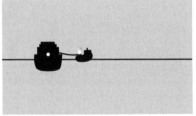

Under Tow (Side Lights): A tugboat shows two vertical masthead lights (three if the tow is over 65 ft.) and a yellow towing light above the stern light, plus the usual sidelights and stern light of a powerboat. The towed vessel shows sidelights and a stern light.

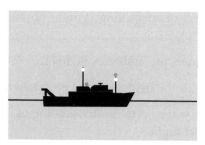

Trawling: A trawler with its trawl out shows powerboat lights plus green over white all-around lights.

Fishing (with nets): A fishing boat with nets shows red over white all-around lights plus normal powerboat lights.

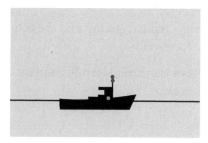

Vessel Not Under Command: Two red all-around lights plus side and stern lights are used. Remember, "Red over red—captain's dead."

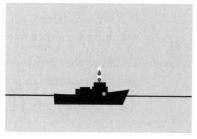

Restricted Maneuverability: Red, white, and red all-around lights plus powerboat lights.

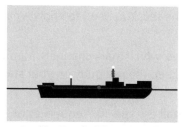

Constrained by Draft: Three red all-around lights plus powerboat lights.

Pilot Boat: White over red all-around lights at masthead plus powerboat lights.

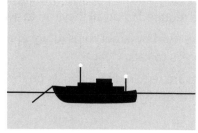

At anchor: Boats over 165 feet have to show two all-around white lights; if under 165 feet, a single white all-around light is required.

Knowing how to identify lights is just one aspect of safe sailing at night. Remember these guidelines as well:

- Your course should be planned in advance, preferably in daylight.

- When going over charts make note of all the lights on your proposed route.

- Sailing in familiar waters will also give you a better understanding of lights and how things can appear differently at night.

- Buoy and boat lights can be difficult to pick out and identify against city lights (traffic, street, buildings etc), so check and double-check the lights you see.

- Having two people on watch (one steering and navigating and the other watching for other boats) is a safer way to travel.

- Be aware that depth perception changes in the dark. Keep binoculars handy and plot or confirm your position frequently.

- Always wear a safety harness at night.

The Least You Need to Know

- Buoys and marks are the street signs of the sea. You need to know what they mean and follow their directions.

- The most common buoys are lateral buoys, which mark channels. Memorizing "red, right, returning" will remind you to keep the red buoy on your starboard side when returning to harbor.

- Lighthouses, buoys, beacons, and ranges all use specific sequences of light flashes so you can recognize them at night. Details are found on your chart or in the U.S. Coast Guard's Light List.

- Rules of the road tell you when to give-way and when to stand-on. All vessels on the water are required to do all they can to avoid collisions.

- Sound signals are used by larger ships to signal their maneuvers. Knowing the signals will help you to keep clear.

- Navigation lights are required by all boats on the water, and each type of boat will have a specific configuration of lights.

Learning the Ropes

In This Chapter

- Selecting the right rope for the right purpose
- Knowing your knots
- Cleating your boat
- Protecting against chafe

The humble rope (whose name mysteriously changes to "line" as soon as it gets near a boat) has a pretty elevated role on a sailboat. We use them to raise, lower, and control sails, to tie up after a day on the water, or to secure things in advance of a blow. The problem is in knowing what rope to choose for what purpose. The choices go beyond double braid, three-strand, eight-strand, and floating, because all of those come in a range of different sizes, breaking strengths, and materials.

Selecting a line isn't as difficult as it might seem (most rope manufacturers have guidelines to help you narrow down your options), but choosing the rope is just the first step. Once you know what you need, you need to get the right amount, learn how to attach it with the correct knot, hitch, or splice, and then care for it so it will last.

There's a reason that entire books (and courses) on rope work are available to sailors. Nothing shows the mark of a novice more than messy lines and incorrectly tied knots. This chapter is an introduction to the basics; but, before you trust your vessel to your new rope works skills, make sure someone more experienced checks over your efforts.

All About Rope

There was a time when rope only came in natural fibers such as cotton, sisal, or hemp, and typically you bought a couple of spools and used them in every application. These days we no longer use just one rope for every purpose; instead it's not unlikely to find a half dozen or more lines of different sizes, materials, and construction on a boat.

When the time comes to purchase new halyards, sheets, dock lines, or anchor rode, it's possible to be overwhelmed by the variety of rope available. The following tables will help you narrow down your choices and choose the right rope. Keep in mind that rope is made by many different manufacturers and comes in different levels of quality. Like anything, sometimes you get what you pay for.

The first step in choosing a rope is knowing which material you need.

Types of Rope

Rope Material	Advantages	Disadvantages	Typical Use
Polypropylene	Light Floats Inexpensive	Weak Poor UV resistance Knots come untied easily	Floating rescue lines
Nylon	Elastic—absorbs shock loads Moderate price	Too stretchy for sail control lines	Anchor, Dock, and Mooring lines
Polyester (double braid construction)	Moderate stretch Moderate price Good UV resistance	Too stretchy for serious racing boats	Best all around rope for running rigging
Spectra/Dyneema	Very strong Very low stretch Abrasion resistant Floats UV resistant	Slippery Expensive	High performance racing yacht running rigging
Kevlar/Aramid/Twaron/Technora	Very strong Very low stretch Moderately Abrasion resistant	UV sensitive Expensive Weakened by knots or tight radius bends	High performance racing yacht running rigging
Vectran	Very strong, very low stretch	Expensive	High performance halyards

Once you've decided on the type of rope you need, you need to decide on the size. Smaller diameter rope tends be less expensive, but it also can be hard to handle. Keep this in mind when you are deciding what you want. Pulling a too-small rope all day can be painful.

Rope Sizes

Boat size:	15'–20'	21'–25'	26'–30'	31'–35'
Anchor or Dock Lines	³⁄₈" nylon	³⁄₈" nylon	¹⁄₂" nylon	⁵⁄₈" nylon
Main Halyard	¹⁄₄" double braid polyester	⁵⁄₁₆" double braid polyester	³⁄₈" double braid polyester	⁷⁄₁₆" double braid polyester
Jib Halyard	¹⁄₄" double braid polyester	⁵⁄₁₆" double braid polyester	³⁄₈" double braid polyester	⁷⁄₁₆" double braid polyester
Spinnaker Halyard	¹⁄₄" double braid polyester	⁵⁄₁₆" double braid polyester	³⁄₈" double braid polyester	⁷⁄₁₆" double braid polyester
Main Sheet	¹⁄₄" double braid polyester	⁵⁄₁₆" double braid polyester	³⁄₈" double braid polyester	⁷⁄₁₆" double braid polyester
Spinnaker Sheets	¹⁄₄" double braid polyester	⁵⁄₁₆" double braid polyester	³⁄₈" double braid polyester	⁷⁄₁₆" double braid polyester
Spinnaker Guys	¹⁄₄" double braid polyester	¹⁄₄" double braid polyester	³⁄₈" double braid polyester	⁷⁄₁₆" double braid polyester
Control Lines (Boom Vang, Foreguy, Topping Lift)	¹⁄₄" double braid polyester	¹⁄₄" double braid polyester	⁵⁄₁₆" double braid polyester	⁵⁄₁₆" double braid polyester

Use these sizes as guidelines. If you already have lines aboard and they are sized correctly for blocks, masthead sheaves, and rigging hardware, it's best to stay with that size.

Rope Words

A rope is a length of heavy cord that, as soon as you actually use it on a boat, is referred to as a line. Typically you would call this former rope by a specific name, as in anchor rode, dock line, or halyard. When working with a rope, keep in mind it has two ends: the *working end* (which you work with, tying knots and such) and the *standing end* (pretty much the rest of the rope).

When you're working with the working end, you can form a *bight*, which is a bend in the rope; a *loop*, which is a full circle; a *hitch*, which attaches it to a post or another object; or a *splice*, which is a method of permanently attaching two parts of a line together; or a knot.

Rope Construction

In the early days of rope making, rope was constructed by spinning short natural fibers into yarns and then taking three yarns and twisting them together in opposite directions to form a rope. Today, three-strand ropes are still constructed this way, typically out of nylon, dacron, or polypropylene. One of the benefits of three-strand rope is it's easy to splice to make into a loop or to *back splice* (a method of braiding the line back into itself) to finish off the end. It also wears well and is stretchy, which makes it a good choice for dock lines or anchor rode.

Three-strand rope is popular for dock lines because of its elasticity.
(Evan Gatehouse)

Double braid has gradually surpassed three-strand for boat use. This type of rope consists of a braided core and a braided cover. Because of the tightly woven cover it has better abrasion resistance than three-strand, and typically the two layers mean the line is stronger. Braided line can also be spliced (though the process is a bit trickier) and it typically holds knots well. The strong point of double braid is its smooth cover; the cover enables it to run easily through pulleys and work well in different types of cleats. It also comes in a range of patterns and colors, making it easy to color code your boat (e.g., the main halyard is blue, the jib halyard is green).

Six-strand and eight-strand ropes are becoming more common for dock lines and anchor rode. Their flexible construction means they fill an anchor rope locker easily and are also quite stretchy.

Double braid rope has a braided inner core and a smooth outer cover, making it a popular choice for rigging lines.

(Evan Gatehouse)

NAUTICAL KNOWLEDGE

The value of having strong ropes is obvious, but the benefits of stretchiness can be confusing. For halyards, sheets, and other rigging lines, stretch is a problem. If you have a stretchy halyard, it means your sail will get looser as the sailing day goes on. The same with your sheets—you'd constantly be tightening them while close hauled. But for dock lines or an anchor rode, elasticity is considered beneficial. It means that when your boat surges against a line, rather than the line breaking (or a cleat getting pulled loose), the line acts like a shock absorber and spreads out the load gradually.

Six Essential Sailing Knots and a Hitch

The phrase "to learn the ropes" is thought to go back to the early days of shipping. When a new sailor came aboard a ship he needed to learn which ropes controlled which sails and he also needed to learn how to tie dozens of different knots and hitches that had purposes that included joining two ropes, making a loop at the end or in the middle of a rope, attaching a rope to the anchor, and more. As you can imagine, learning the ropes was a complex and time-consuming process.

In modern sailing we have a wide range of different kinds of shackles, rope clutches, and cleats, which means that a number of the old-time knots have become obsolete. But while modern hardware has replaced some of the more complicated knots, there are still six knots and at least one hitch that every sailor should know.

SAILOR'S WARNING

When a knot is tied, the rope fibers become kinked, stretched, twisted, and broken, and this can weaken rope up to 50 percent, depending on the type of knot and the rope. Older, stiffer rope fairs more poorly in tests of knot/rope strength, so make sure you're using rope that provides an adequate safety factor. For important loads, a good safety factor means the rope's breaking strength should be six times the load (6:1).

Figure Eight Knot

A figure eight knot is used as a stopper knot—a knot tied in the end of a line to keep the line from sliding past a fitting or being pulled out of sight. Commonly found at the base of the mast or in the ends of sheets (though never for spinnaker sheets), figure eights are used because they don't bind. Even after a figure eight has been jammed tightly against a block, it can be easily undone. This also means figure eights can come undone unexpectedly, so keep an eye on them and retie them as required.

Here's how to tie a figure eight knot:

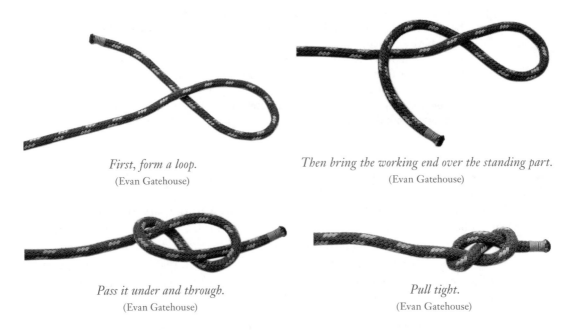

First, form a loop.
(Evan Gatehouse)

Then bring the working end over the standing part.
(Evan Gatehouse)

Pass it under and through.
(Evan Gatehouse)

Pull tight.
(Evan Gatehouse)

Reef Knot

A reef knot is used for tying two ropes of the same size together. It's often used for tying mainsail reefing lines together or anything else that doesn't need a permanent knot. The reef knot is easy to undo by gripping one loose end, and pulling it back over the knot in the opposite direction.

Here's how to tie a reef knot:

Holding one end of each line in each hand, pass the left line over the right and tuck under.
(Evan Gatehouse)

Then pass the right line over the left ...
(Evan Gatehouse)

... and tuck under.
(Evan Gatehouse)

Bowline

A bowline (pronounced *bow lin*, not bow line) is an easy way to make a loop in a line that can be used for tying sheets to a jib clew or securing a dinghy's *painter* to a dock or boat. It is quick to tie (once you practice), doesn't slip, and doesn't jam.

DEFINITION

A **painter** is a line used on the bow of a dinghy to secure it to a dock or a boat.

There is a popular mnemonic used to teach the bowline that involves a rabbit. Here's how to tie a bowline knot, using the mnemonic:

Form a loop and imagine that's the rabbit hole, and the end of the rope is the rabbit.
(Evan Gatehouse)

The rabbit comes up the hole …
(Evan Gatehouse)

… runs around the tree …
(Evan Gatehouse)

… and hops back down the hole.
(Evan Gatehouse)

Clove Hitch

A clove hitch is used for temporarily securing a line around a rail or other cylindrical object. It's used to hang fenders to the boat's rails, and some people use it for tying a dinghy to a dock. (Personally, I'd use a round turn and two half hitches.) Clove hitches can easily be adjusted or undone.

Here's how to tie a clove hitch:

Wrap the working end of a length of rope around the object bringing it back over the top of the standing end.
(Evan Gatehouse)

As the end comes around the second time, tuck it under itself.
(Evan Gatehouse)

Round Turn and Two Half Hitches

A round turn and two half hitches is a better choice than a bowline for tying up a line to a dock. It's easy to untie when it's under load.

Here's how to tie a round turn and two half hitches:

Wrap the working end of a length of rope completely around the object.
(Evan Gatehouse)

Cross over, and tuck it under. This is the first half hitch.
(Evan Gatehouse)

Cross over again, and tuck to make the second half hitch. With slippery line you can add an extra half hitch.
(Evan Gatehouse)

Sheet Bend

A sheet bend is used for tying two ropes together. It works well for two ropes of uneven size if you make the loop out of the larger line.

Here's how to tie a sheet bend:

Use two ropes. Make a bight in the larger of the ropes. Bring the second rope up and around the bight.
(Evan Gatehouse)

Tuck the smaller rope under itself and pull tight.
(Evan Gatehouse)

You can make the knot more secure by wrapping the smaller rope around the loop twice, making it a double sheet bend.
(Evan Gatehouse)

The Cleat Hitch

When you tie your boat to a dock after docking, you're cleating it. Often when you pull into a slip you'll tie up temporarily and then adjust your lines so that the boat is lying parallel to the side of the dock. Once your boat is adjusted, secure the bow and stern lines to the dock cleats with a cleat hitch. You should already have used the cleat hitch to secure the lines to your boat's cleats.

Here's how to make a cleat hitch:

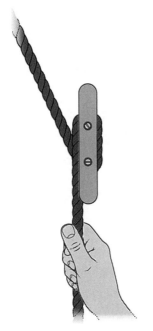

*Holding the working end of the line,
wrap once around the cleat.*

*Cross the line across the cleat, passing it
around the horn in a figure eight. Continue
this way or complete it with a locking hitch.*

To finish the cleat with a locking hitch, flip over the last half of the figure eight so the line runs parallel to the first figure eight.
(Evan Gatehouse)

BETTER BOATING

Many smaller boats don't have a mid-ship cleat on the boat's sidedeck to attach the dock lines to. So, if want you want to tie lines from the boat's center, tie them to the chainplate. Use a round turn and two half hitches to secure both the forward and aft lines and then cleat the other end at the dock.

SAILOR'S WARNING

Never tie dock lines to stanchions; they are not made to withstand the loads produced by the boat moving forward and aft and will break, bend, or start to leak under the load.

Storing Rope

When ropes are not in use, they should be coiled and hung up to keep them from being in the way. Coiling lines also helps keep them from getting dirty and tangled. Braided rope is coiled slightly differently than three-strand, but the goal is to end up with coils all the same length that can be locked off with a loop and hitch.

When storing coils of halyards and sheets, hang them from mast cleats or winches or set up a hanging system in your cockpit. Lines that aren't in regular use should be hung up in a locker out of the sun.

Here's how to properly coil and store a rope:

To prevent kinks, three-strand rope is given a slight turn with each loop. Despite the turn, braided rope often will form a figure eight, but that's fine.

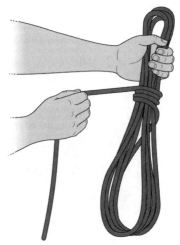

When you have finished coiling most of the line and have two coils worth left, wrap this end around the coils several times.

Make a loop with the remaining end and push it through the coils above your wrap.

Bring the loop over the top of the coil and pull the end tight. This will give you a tail to secure the coil to a hanging surface.

Protecting Against Chafe

When it comes to rope failure, age and sun exposure both play a role, but the major culprit is *chafe*. Chafe occurs when lines rub against just about anything (even each other) and the friction of the rubbing wears through the strands of rope.

The solution is twofold: first, you should try to reroute lines so they run freely without friction, and second, you need to provide chafe protection. Chafe gear is typically some sort of sacrificial protection such as fire hose, garden hose, bicycle-tire inner tube, or a commercial product that slips over your line and protects it at the spot where it was chafing.

Tips for avoiding chafe:

- Check for chafe. Dock lines and anchor rode are the two primary types of lines that chafe, but also check your roller furler lines, halyards, and sheets for signs of damage.

- Reroute the lines. Blocks and fairleads are designed to help you run your lines with a minimum of friction. You can add blocks for moving lines (sheets and halyards) and fairleads for stationary lines (dock lines and anchor rode).

Tips for procuring and installing chafe gear:

- Choose chafe gear that is large enough to fit over the line and small enough to fit through the fitting. You may need different types of protection for different lines.

- Make sure chafe gear fits and will stay in place. It's not just diameter that matters—you need to have enough protection that as the line moves, the chafe gear protects the entire length of line that was rubbing.

The Least You Need to Know

- Selecting the right rope means choosing the right construction, material, and size for a given use.
- There are six essential knots and one hitch that every sailor should know. They are easy to learn, but take practice to get correct.

- If your boat doesn't have a mid-ship cleat on the sidedeck, you can cleat securely to the dock by attaching the line to the chainplate instead.
- Caring for your lines means coiling them, keeping them tidy, and protecting them against chafe.

Leaving Her Shipshape

In This Chapter

- Cleaning up after a day on the water
- Doing regular maintenance
- Hauling your boat for bottom painting
- Winterizing your boat

After a day on the water, you've safely docked and securely tied up your boat (see Chapter 12) and it's time to head home. Wait! Hopefully you've returned to the dock with an hour or so of daylight to spare, because remember that predeparture checklist from Chapter 5? Well, you're going to want to do roughly the reverse of that (plus a few things) before leaving your boat.

Before you say, no worries, that you'll be back tomorrow, keep in mind stuff happens. A few years ago a neighbouring boat pulled in near us. It was late in the day, so they left the boat as is with the plan of returning in the morning. Windows were open; the mainsail was uncovered; vital gear was left on deck. Days passed; rains came; and a storm blew through and despite the efforts of other people at the dock to better secure things, the lovely boat was damaged.

It turned out a family emergency had pulled the owners away. By the time they returned, the boat was a mess inside and out. Open windows meant a lot of water got into the cabin. Some electronics were ruined and the mainsail was damaged. The moral is pretty simple: an hour spent tidying up the boat could have saved the owners a lot of work and future expense.

Clean and Secure

Whenever you bring the boat back to the dock, you'll want to leave it so that it'll be in much the same shape when you return. What this means in reality is you'll want to start by washing down the boat. (This also gives you a great chance to inspect everything as you go.) There are loads of special boat cleaners on the market, but many of them contain harsh chemicals—all of which get washed directly into the ocean:

- Phosphates found in cleaners cause oxygen depletion, which can result in damage to aquatic life.

- Cleaning products that contain chlorine, ammonia, potassium hydroxide, and solvents are harmful to sea life.

- Degreasers are drying and can reduce the natural oils that fish need for their gills to take in oxygen.

- Many chemical cleaners contain hormone disruptors, which can damage the reproductive cycle of fish.

- Dust and other cleaning residue can lead to increased waterborne particulates, decreasing the amount of sunlight penetrating the water and inhibiting photosynthesis.

So when you're cleaning up, keep the environment in mind.

Exterior Cleaning

Chances are you won't need to do everything on the following list every single time you use your boat. But you will want to make sure you keep your boat salt and grime free as much as possible.

Green cleaning tips:

- Wash the exterior of your boat by hand using fresh water. Remember: more frequent cleaning with less potent cleaners is kinder to the environment.

- Choose a long-handled deck brush for washing the deck. But don't skip the hard-to-reach areas. A smaller scrub brush or a rag or two are also handy.

- Use phosphate-free, biodegradable detergents and cleaning compounds when you do need added cleaning power.

- When cleaning stainless steel (such as stanchions or chain plates), try using water and a green scrubby to remove rust. If the stains are really stubborn, try baking soda.

- If you do have wood trim on the exterior of your boat, skip traditional teak cleaners (when possible) and try washing with water. If you maintain the finish, you won't need to strip and clean the wood as often.

- Wash sails with fresh water once or twice a season. This is especially important if they managed to get wet with salt spray. To rinse them, hoist them on a calm sunny day and spray them with fresh water. Let them dry before packing them away. Don't use chlorine bleach on sails.

- Soak sheets and lines in a bucket of fresh water that contains a cup of vinegar and then dry them thoroughly. They only need this if they've become salty or if you're finding that they're becoming stiff.

- Wax the hull and cabin sides once or twice a season to help protect the paint or gelcoat finish. (Never put wax on the deck—it will make it really slippery.)

- Wash canvas *dodgers*, *biminis*, or covers with water and a mild biodegradable laundry soap. Either use your scrub brush to work in the solution, or use a cloth to wipe things down. Rinse well.

DEFINITION

A **dodger** is roughy equivlant to a car's front windshield and provides protection to the front of the cockpit and companionway opening from wind, rain, or spray. Made of canvas and with a clear vinyl window to see through, dodgers can make sailing in inclement weather more comfortable.

A **bimini** is an awning that covers some or all of a cockpit and protects you from the sun or rain. Made of canvas, many biminis are only used when a boat is moored because they interfere with the mainsail.

- To avoid scratching, first rinse clear vinyl windows found on dodgers or enclosures to remove the salt and loosen grime. Next clean them using a soft cloth (not a paper towel, these can scratch, too) and a weak water-and-vinegar solution.

- Some marinas require that you to take your boat out of the water and move it to a contained area for scraping, sanding, and painting. If you stay at the dock, make sure to capture and properly dispose of the residue.

Interior Cleaning

Cleaning the interior of a boat isn't much different than cleaning the exterior. The goal is to remove salt (which can cause corrosion in your electronics and encourage mildew growth) and keep a good eye on the condition of everything. Try to unpack lockers now and again and be sure to lift the floorboards regularly. Do the following:

- Wipe down the bulkheads and inside cupboards with a solution of water and vinegar. This will usually stop any mildew growth.

- Take home any items (cushions, foul-weather gear, and bedding) that may have become wet with saltwater for a thorough cleaning. Left alone, salt will continue to attract moisture and can lead to mildew growth.

- Tip up cushions so the air will circulate around them.

- Take home garbage and recycling.

- Wash and dry all the dishes you used. Take the dish towels home for laundering.

- Use reusable cloths, rags, or towels, rather than disposable paper towels.

- Keep your interior woodwork looking good with regular applications of lemon oil or a regular varnishing routine.

- Replace harsh toilet cleaners with baking soda and a brush.

- If you use the boat frequently, every few months pump $\frac{1}{2}$ gallon of vinegar through your head's hoses and let it sit for several hours or overnight. This breaks down deposits and helps your plumbing last longer.

- Arrange to have your holding tank pumped out when required.

- Clean your bilges. Use an oil-absorbing pad if there is any chance of fuel in your bilge and then wipe down your bilges with a vinegar-and-water solution. Some moisture in bilges tends to be normal, but by keeping your bilges clean and dry you'll know if you have a leak.

Developing a Maintenance Routine

As you tidy up your boat, inspect things as you wash them down and put them away. Look your sails over for pin holes, small tears, and damaged stitching after you've washed them and before you cover them up. Check your lines and sheets for chafe and excessive stiffness as you coil and store them away. As you shut hatches and windows, make sure the gaskets are sealing properly and that you are able to securely dog them (fasten them closed). When you close the seacocks, make sure they shut smoothly, the hoses are in good shape, and the hose clamps are secure.

You might find it handy to keep a routine maintenance log in the front of a log book. This way you know when you last checked things and can also make plans for future maintenance.

Depending on the complexity and age of your boat, every maintenance list will look a little different, but this example list may give you some ideas.

Engine and Fuel System

An inboard engine is probably the most complex and expensive piece of equipment on your boat, so it makes sense to check it after or before every use. If you don't have an engine manual on hand, you'll want to get one so you know about your engine's specific needs.

Be sure to check the following:

- Check fluid levels on nonsealed batteries and top them up with distilled water as required.

- Check the primary fuel filter; often this has a clear bowl so you can see if it contains any water or sediment.

- Inspect engine oil, transmission fluid, and coolant for correct levels and for contamination.

- Inspect the engine cooling water intake sea strainer; this tends to have a clear lid and is easy to inspect.

- Inspect the water pump impeller; these are made of rubber or neoprene and they break down over time. Most engine manuals have a recommended schedule for replacement but you'll want to check it now and again— especially if you had any stoppage in the flow of cooling water.

The impeller pump forces water through the engine, but if it becomes worn or damaged your engine can overheat.

- Inspect the fuel line for leaks or damage. Look at the hose clamps to make sure they're secure and check that there are no bulges or kinks in the hose.

- Inspect hoses and the alternator belts for wear. Belts should be adequately tight (but still possible to push with your thumb) but shouldn't be loose enough to slip.

- For outboard motors, schedule an annual service call to make sure that your motor is in good running order. But having an owner's manual and spares aboard is good practice.

BETTER BOATING

Check with your marina or city for directions on where to recycle spent antifreeze, fuel, fuel-absorbing cloths, oil, oil filters, and batteries. Don't just dump these items into the trash after you have performed maintenance.

Dinghy

It's easy to forget, but if you rely on a dinghy don't wait until you need it to check its condition. You probably only need to check your dinghy once a season or if you notice a problem, but check the following:

- Check your inflatable dinghy to make sure they it holds air. Remember in warmer conditions (midday or summer) air expands, so your dinghy may seem a bit deflated on cool mornings.

- Make sure both oars and the oar locks are in good condition.

- Check your safety equipment. A bailer, anchor, waterproof VHF, and first aid kit are all good things to have aboard a dinghy but should be put away when not in use.

Interior

Check over the inside of your boat every time you use it. Typically this is done as you clean up and close it after use:

- Make sure windows, hatches, vents, etc. are sealing properly.

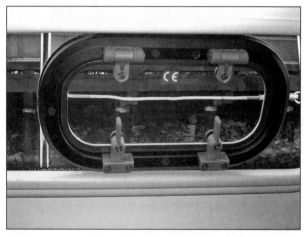

Hatches and ports should be inspected for signs of leaking.
(Evan Gatehouse)

- Look for hidden signs of dampness or leaks in lockers and bilges.
- Ensure the fridge is cleaned out and the drain plug is removed.
- Shut through-hulls to test the valves for smooth functioning.
- Make sure bilge pumps are on and functioning.
- Test interior lights and replace burned-out bulbs.
- Inspect wiring for signs of corrosion or other damage.

Deck and Topsides

As part of your cleaning routine you'll want to make weekly, monthly, or seasonal checks of these items:

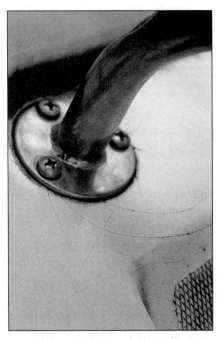

Crazing at the base of this stanchion and a dent further up mean this stanchion should be watched for leaks and tightened, if needed.
(Evan Gatehouse)

- Check stanchion bases for looseness or signs of damage.
- Note any cracking or crazing of the gelcoat, especially around cleats, stanchion bases, the mast base, and chainplates.
- Inspect canvas for required repairs, damaged stitching, or corroded fasteners.
- Check lifelines for damaged coverings and loose wires.
- Ensure that running and anchor lights are working and bulbs aren't burned out.
- Inspect rigging for missing cotter pins, broken wires, and cracked turnbuckles. Arrange for a full rig inspection if anything concerns you.

- Check all lines, halyards, and sheets for chafing.

- Spin the winches to check that they move smoothly. If they don't, arrange to strip and service them.

Electronics and Safety

Safety is important, so be sure to check your electronics and PFDs on a regular basis. You don't need to do a thorough inspection every time you sail, but you should become familiar enough with the items so you can detect wear or damage:

- Bring all portable electronic and safety items in from outside.

- Remove batteries from portable devices and check wiring for corrosion and wear. Make sure they are clean and dry before storing them away.

- Check the condition of the fabric, zippers and buckles, and sizes of your PFDs, especially if you are boating with children. Give them a fresh water rinse if they got salty.

Hauling Out

Hauling out is a general term for pulling your boat out of the water and putting it in a yard on the hard. Depending on how you store your boat, you'll either be pulling it out of the water frequently (if you store it on a trailer or it's a dinghy) or annually (if you keep it at a dock).

Typically a haul out is done in the spring (unless you store your boat on the hard over winter). The reason for hauling in the spring is so your paint is fresh as the weather is warming up. To get a boat out of the water, boatyards use marine railways, trailers or, most commonly, a *travel lift*.

Watching your boat get picked up by a travel lift for the first time is an unnerving experience. Slings are fitted under your bow and stern and then your boat is hoisted from the water. Next your boat is power washed and then driven to a spot in the yard where it is propped up with jack stands until the work is complete and it goes back into the water.

As you can imagine, your boat is going to go through some motion that is not that typical for it when it's hauled out. So before you get lifted up, go through your boat and put away items that might get broken or come loose during the haul out. Also clean off your decks of items that might fall off our get damaged by the slings.

Travel lifts lower their slings into the water and boats maneuver into them. Once secured, the boat is lifted into the air and transported to a place on land.
(Evan Gatehouse)

Washing and Inspecting

The first thing that should happen after your boat is lifted out of the water is the hull should be pressure-washed. It's really important to do this before any growth dries and the weed and slime become hard to remove. As the yard workers spray your boat, watch carefully; make sure they also knock off any mussels or barnacles. If some of the old bottom paint flakes off as they wash, ask the yard worker to go around again; you want to remove all the loose paint before putting on the next coat.

BETTER BOATING

Check if the boatyard you are planning to use has an effective environmental management plan in place. Boatyards can be a haven for toxic chemicals, and poor environmental practices can mean chemicals end up in the ocean or in landfills. Ask how the boatyard minimizes the risk of soil and water contamination or simply look for a yard that is part of the Clean Marinas Program (cleanmarina.org).

Once you're propped up on the jack stands, it's time to inspect things under the waterline. Look the hull over for impact marks, cracks, and blisters, and arrange for their repair before you paint. Check the condition of the rudder and keel. Check the propeller and shaft. Wiggle the shaft and see if the bearings are loose. (Very slight movement is normal.) Look for corroded through hull fittings, and retest your seacocks. (This would be the time for replacement.)

Renew all *zincs*. The way you protect underwater metal parts (propellers and shafts, for example) on a boat from corrosion is by using sacrificial zinc anodes. Keep in mind that for a zinc anode to be effective, it must be in physical contact with the metal being protected. Also don't paint the zinc; it won't work unless the metal is exposed. Depending on your marina and your boat, zincs will corrode at different rates, but if your zinc anodes are disappearing rapidly, be sure to consult a marine electrician.

Painting

If you store your boat in the water, chances are you'll use some sort of *antifouling* or bottom paint. Generally you have a choice between a hard paint, which gradually loses efficacy, or a soft, ablative paint that wears away. Choosing the right paint for your boat depends on your location, the temperature of your water, how much you want to spend, and how you'll be using your boat. Ask at your marina or your local marine store about which paint is most popular for your area. Keep in mind that much of a paint's effectiveness comes from how well you prepped your boat before you apply the paint, so follow the manufacturer's directions.

 DEFINITION

Antifouling paint is a coating that is applied to the underside of a sailboat to inhibit weed and barnacle growth. (Weeds slow a boat down.)

Once you've completed any repairs, it's time to prep for painting. Be sure to read through all manufacturer directions and assemble all the correct protective safety equipment (gloves and a paint suit to keep the paint off your skin and a respirator and ear plugs if you're sanding first) and painting supplies (paint, rollers, brushes, tape, tray, solvent) before beginning.

Before repainting the hull, you need to be sure there is no loose or flaking paint and that the new paint has an uncontaminated surface to adhere to. This may mean stripping the old paint, but generally sanding will be sufficient.

SAILOR'S WARNING

Antifouling paint is toxic, so wear disposable coveralls, gloves, and eye protection.

You can either wet sand, using special wet and dry sand paper and running water, or you can use a power sander. (This must be fitted with a dust capture bag.) Your goal is to sand away most of the previous application so you can avoid the kind of thick build-up that eventually flakes off. Many sailors use a different color of paint each year to help determine when they have sanded enough.

BETTER BOATING

Before your haul out, check to see when you need your next insurance survey. They are not necessary every year, but it makes sense to have your insurance survey done while you are already hauled out.

Tape around the *boot stripe* (the line where bottom paint and topside paint meet) using an appropriate masking tape. Then using well-mixed paint (if you bought it a while ago make sure you have it shaken or use a power drill mixer before application) begin rolling the paint onto the hull using a short-nap roller cover.

We like to start on one side at the bow and work our way around the boat, trying to avoid painting in direct sunlight when we can. Add thinner to your paint only if the manufacturer directions say so and then use only the thinner that is specified.

Add a second coat when the directions say so and get someone from the yard to shift the jack stands when the paint is hard enough so you can paint those areas. (Never try to move the jack stands yourself.) Be sure to save some of the paint to get the areas on the bottom of the keel for when they lift your boat.

Longer-Term Storage

Depending on where you live, chances are there will be a few months each year when you don't use your boat and you'll need to winterize it. You may live in a place like the Northeast, where you haul it out and leave it on the hard, or if you are in a milder climate it may be warm enough to leave it in the water. If you are leaving your boat on the hard, many marinas offer complete winterization packages and can save you the work.

Wherever you keep your boat through the winter, make sure you check on it regularly. Especially after storms, cold snaps, heavy rain, or heavy snow. Your preparations will go a long way toward protecting your boat, but if something occurs you want to be checking on things frequently enough so that a problem doesn't sit unresolved for long.

For the most part you will be following your general finished-boating-for-the-day list when it comes to leaving the boat clean and secure. But winterizing also includes a few additional steps that can take several hours. Here are the main areas to cover:

- Exterior: Remove sails if possible. This is a great time to send them off to the sailmaker for inspection and repair. Otherwise rinse them with fresh water, dry them thoroughly, and store them away in a dry location. If you can't remove them, secure your roller furling with extra wraps by taking the sheets out of the leads and wrapping them around the sail.

  Also add extra ties to the mainsail and ensure the sail cover is over all parts of the sail. Take in all the exterior cushions and wash them and store them somewhere dry. Remove any canvas bimini or dodger and store it so that the vinyl windows are kept flat. If you have any hatches or ports that leak, secure a tarp over the boom to help keep things dry.

- Inboard Engine: Change the oil and oil filter as well as the transmission fluid. (Note this in your log book so you remember you did it in the spring.) Flush the cooling system with antifreeze. This will vary from engine to engine, so follow the specific guidelines for your engine. For the now rare gas inboard engines, remove the spark plugs and spray fogging oil into each cylinder. Finish up by wiping down the entire engine. And ensure all seacocks are closed.

- Outboard Engine: Run the outboard in a tank or bucket filled with fresh water to flush it. Disconnect the fuel hose and run the engine until it stops. Wipe down the engine and let it dry. Remove the spark plugs and spray with fogging oil and do the same with the cylinder walls and pistons. Change the gear oil in the lower unit. Then store the engine upright in a dry location.

- Fuel: Leave fuel tanks either completely empty or completely full to avoid condensation build up caused by the cold weather. If you leave them full, using a fuel stabilizer is recommended.

- Bilges: After cleaning the bilges, splash in a little nontoxic antifreeze inside the bilge area to keep any water that gets in from freezing.

- Fresh Water Tanks: Drain the tanks by running the faucets dry. Then close off the faucets and refill the system with a nontoxic antifreeze. Turn on all the faucets one by one until you see the pink antifreeze coming out.

- Head: Have the holding tank pumped and flushed multiple times. Follow the manufacturer's directions for the correct method of winterizing.

- Interior: If you can, take home items such as cushions, charts, books, electronics, etc. this is the best place for them. Once you've removed what you can, open all cupboards and drawers so the air can circulate. Consider using a dehumidifier to keep things dry. But don't run a heater unattended as this could be a fire hazard.

Before leaving, double-check that you have closed all sea cocks, turned on the bilge pump, and made sure the battery was fully charged.

Out on the dock, double-check your dock lines. Add additional lines, fenders, and chafe protection if you are in a stormy climate and expect rough weather.

The Least You Need to Know

- Whenever you leave your boat, you should leave it clean and secure.
- Developing a maintenance routine where you become familiar with all aspects of your boat will help you recognize problems before they become serious.
- Boats that are kept in the water typically require an annual haul out so you can apply bottom paint and change the zinc anodes.
- Winterizing a boat means preparing it to be left for a longer period of time. Depending on the type of boat you have and the climate, this may be a lengthy process.

Common Basic Repairs

In This Chapter

- Repairing minor fiberglass damage
- Finding and repairing leaks
- Installing new electronics
- Replacing a halyard
- Replacing an impeller

When you own a boat, you'll have the weekly, monthly, and annual boat maintenance projects such as changing oil and filters, looking for chafe on lines and sails, greasing bits and pieces, and painting the bottom. And then you'll also have the unexpected problems—when things break or stop working.

While you probably bought your boat with the intent to sail it, maintaining it is also part of the deal. One option is to buy a new boat that's under warranty and budget for someone else to do the nonwarranty work. But most boat owners soon realize that hiring someone else to do basic repair work is pretty impractical.

A do-it-yourself attitude is simply part of sailing. The good news is most tasks are pretty straightforward and they don't take too many specialized skills or tools, and some of them are even fun. And keep in mind that just like everything else to do with sailboats, there are often classes available to help you learn the basics in fiberglassing, plumbing, engine maintenance, and even wiring for 12 volts. The following tasks aren't the only ones you'll run into on a boat, but they do represent a few of the more common projects that come up.

Repairing Fiberglass

Fiberglass is pretty sturdy stuff, which is one reason that it's a popular choice for boats. Another reason is it's pretty easy to repair. That ding in the hull that marks the first time you tried docking in a cross-wind? Or the chunk out of your deck where something heavy got dropped? And even the place you drilled for a new cleat (then realized you measured wrong): all repairable.

Keep in mind what we're talking about here are small, nonstructural cosmetic repairs. Typically they're not urgent (unless you've penetrated the core and water is seeping in), but they can cost hundreds of dollars to be professionally repaired. If repairs are structural in nature, or penetrate multiple layers of fiberglass, you might want to get a professional to tackle the repair.

To repair scratches, dings, and gouges in fiberglass, start off by cleaning the area with acetone to remove any wax, grease, and dirt. Then you'll want to expose new material. The goal with a damaged area is to open up the crack or crunch just enough to expose enough new material to apply filler to. A Dremel tool with a variety of attachments will make the job go quickly if you have a number of scars.

Cleaning up this heavily gouged area meant sanding a larger area to expose new material.
(Evan Gatehouse)

To make the repair, select a grinding attachment slightly wider than the crack, and while wearing eye protection, gently grind away the old material to create a shallow V-shape. Then fair the edges into the rest of the hull. Fairing compounds have some shrinkage and hard edges may lead to a hairline crack.

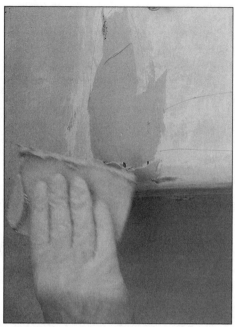

Using a premixed filler, spread the repair material over the damaged area.
(Evan Gatehouse)

When you have completed grinding the damaged spots, clean away all dust and wipe down with a solvent. Premixed fillers such as 3M's Premium Marine Filler are easier and faster to work with than mix-it-yourself epoxies, although they do cost more. Mix small batches of filler and apply with an oversized flexible spreader. Spread evenly over the void, ensuring there are no air spaces or low spots. It often works best to overfill the area so it can be sanded smooth when dry.

After the filler has hardened, sand the area with 80- to 150-grit sandpaper. Always use protective gear like respirators and goggles during sanding.

The final step is to apply a color topcoating with a *gelcoat* repair kit. Gelcoat is a thick pigmented glossy resin that forms the outer surface of a fiberglass boat. Kits are available with tints so you can match the repair to your boat color. When the gelcoat has hardened, sand with increasing higher grades of wet and dry sandpaper starting at 400-grit and increasing to 1,200. Then buff the repair with a polishing compound. It's hard to match gelcoat colors perfectly, even for professionals, so don't despair if your repair is slightly visible. Very small holes or dings can be filled with just gelcoat alone. And if your boat has been previously painted, painting the well-sanded repair is also an option.

Sand the area smooth until the filled area is level with the surrounding hull.
(Evan Gatehouse)

Matching the paint to the surrounding area can be tricky, but after it's buffed with wax, it tends to blend in.
(Evan Gatehouse)

Locating a Deck Leak

Boats leak. They are large, flexible structures that experience considerable stresses and loads. Most of these loads occur at the points where hardware is attached to the deck. As time goes on, the sealant compound used to bed the hardware loses flexibility and breaks down, then the deck flexes just enough to break the seal, and one day you notice water running down an inside bulkhead.

The problem with leaks is that, unless you're lucky, the point where water first penetrates the deck or cabin structure is rarely close to the place where the annoying drip finally emerges inside the cabin. Once the water breaches the top skin of the fiberglass, it travels the path of least resistance. This means the water can travel along the core or it may take a detour through the interior liner before it makes an appearance inside the cabin. So, the first step in fixing a leak is to find the leak. Do the following:

- Use your eyes. Leaky fittings often rust around their edges above deck, or weep rust below deck. If nothing is obvious, then the next step is to check the slope of the deck around where you see the leak and try to isolate the most likely culprits.

- Give it the hose. Have one person up on deck with a hose and one person below watching the leak. Starting at the lowest possible leak source (based on deck slope) and working your way up, spray each piece of hardware for a minute or two, continuing until the person below sees water appear.

- Write on your boat. Have a persistent wet bunk but you never seem to be around while it's raining to find out where the water is coming from? Draw a series of horizontal lines with a washable marker on the inside of your cabin, starting from the wet area and moving upward. Rainwater running down the cabin sides will leave a track through the lines, leading you upward to the source of water entry.

Repairing Common Leaks

In most cases, once you've located a leak, the next step is to repair it. Following are common leaks and their recommended fixes.

Pre-Existing Holes

Many boats have small holes that were drilled into the deck and never repaired properly. Often they are filled with putty or caulking, which over time cracks and loosens. These holes may be quite obvious or they might be hidden under deck hardware.

The Fix: The first step is to dig out all the old caulking and drill a slightly larger hole to expose new material. Check the core to make sure it is dry. If there is minor dampness, dig out that core material from between the upper and lower fiberglass skins. Clean the area with acetone and then securely tape over the bottom of the hole. Slowly fill the hole with thickened epoxy. Afterward apply a dot of paint on the cured resin to match the gelcoat color as best you can. (Gelcoat doesn't stick well to cured epoxy.)

Hatches, Windows, and Ports

Hatches, windows, and ports often begin to leak over time. Before you look for other causes, first check the gasket. If the gasket is old, it won't compress and seal. Then check for hatch dogs (the lever that closes the hatch) or hinges that go through the lens. Some dogs have O-rings that allow the dog to rotate. Remove the dog and relubricate the O-ring with silicone grease.

Another cause of leaking hatches and ports is when the caulking that the hatch is bedded in has hardened with age. It can be difficult to isolate these leaks if the builder has installed the inside frame of the hatch or port over top of the cabin liner. When this type of installation begins to leak, the water wicks under the liner and into the cabin, making it difficult to pinpoint the leak.

The least likely reason for a leak is the caulking that holds the hatch pane in place has failed. This is usually an obvious leak to find and it's best to consult the manufacturer for a repair.

More serious, some leaks happen because the underlying deck or cabin structure is not strong enough to support the opening. If you repair a hatch or window frame leak and discover that it quickly reappears, consult a surveyor or naval architect for additional advice.

The Fix: If water is leaking in from under the hatch or window frame, you'll need to unbolt the entire assembly. Next, carefully wedge or cut the frame from the hole (or use a debonding agent such as Marine Formula to get the adhesive to release). Then scrape off the old caulking from the deck and frame.

Use a slightly oversized drill bit and drill out the fastener holes. Make sure the core has been sealed with thickened epoxy. If unsealed core is visible, dig it out to a depth of $\frac{3}{8}$ of an inch and fill the space with thickened epoxy. Be sure to fill the bolt or screw holes with epoxy, too. When the epoxy is set, put the hatch or port in place and drill for the fasteners.

Tape off the surrounding deck and hatch frame with masking tape. It's been said that you can tell the professionals from the amateurs by how much masking tape they use. Caulking has an uncanny ability to spread itself where it doesn't belong, so use lots of tape. Then caulk the hatch and deck with a generous amount of marine caulking. (Check the hatch manufacturer for the correct type.)

Typical caulking options for a boat are silicone, polysulphide, polyurethane, and polyether:

- Silicones: This is a good choice for isolating dissimilar metals, but the bond is not as strong as the other choices. It is compatible with most plastics.

- Polysulphide: Probably the most versatile of the caulking options. It can be sanded and painted after it is cured, but don't use it with plastics. 3M 101 or Lifecaulk are common brands.

- Polyurethane: The common choice here is 3M's 5200 or Sikaflex 291. It forms a very strong bond and is used by boat builders to attach the deck to the hull. Avoid use on plastics because it will melt ABS and Lexan. The strength of the bond means it can be very difficult to remove the hardware.

- Polyether: These newer sealants are weaker than polyurethanes but are very weather resistant. West Marine Multi Caulk or 3M 4000 UV Polyether sealant are examples.

After caulking, set the hatch or port in place and bolt it down without fully tightening the bolts. Only after the caulking has set and formed a waterproof gasket (usually the next day) should you tighten the bolts fully.

Chainplates

Chainplates are hard to make leak proof. These hefty chunks of stainless steel penetrate the brittle fiberglass of the deck and then are attached to a wooden bulkhead or the fiberglass hull. The force on the chainplates is immense, and because they tend to move a bit under load, most will start leaking over time.

The Fix: For typical minor leaks, you don't need to remove the chainplate. Your goal is simply to seal up the point where the metal passes through the deck. To do this, remove any cover plate (this is probably easiest to do by first undoing the shroud, but only do one at a time!) and dig out all the old caulk. Then clean the fiberglass surface by sanding it or grinding with a Dremel tool.

Then fill the rectangular hole around the chainplate with an adhesive such as Lifecaulk. Once the caulking has cured, you may need to add a final bead of caulk and reattach the rectangular cover plate.

Stanchions and Deck Hardware

Every time that visiting guests heave themselves up onto your deck while using your *stanchion* for leverage, they're increasing the possibility that the deck will spring a leak where it is attached. Many stanchions simply have too small of a base or inadequate backing plates to withstand that sort of normal-seeming pressure.

> **DEFINITION**
>
> **Stanchions** are the metal posts supporting the lifelines around the deck.

With deck hardware, most leaks are found under hardware that was badly installed, or at unrepaired holes left from old hardware when it was replaced with new hardware.

The Fix: Deck hardware and stanchion base leaks can be fixed in much the same manner that deck leaks are repaired. Some boats are constructed so that these items are attached to solid fiberglass and not cored deck. If this is the case, you'll be able to skip a few steps. Filling the holes with epoxy and then redrilling them to the proper size is only required if the deck is cored.

To help make fasteners leak proof, drill with a countersink bit on the deck at the fastener hole. This leaves space for some additional caulking to form an O-ring of sealant around the fastener that won't be squeezed out when you bolt down the hardware.

An important additional step is to include a backing plate if there wasn't one already. The backing plate helps to distribute the forces and it should be made of aluminum, stainless steel, or fiberglass. Make backing plates bigger than the footprint of the hardware on deck. The thickness of backing plates should be about one half the diameter of the bolts. Avoid plywood because it can compress or rot.

Replacing Electronics

On a small boat, with one or two batteries, the 12-volt electrical system is usually pretty simple: you'll have a battery that is charged by an alternator, possibly a battery charger, and a breaker panel that distributes power from the battery to the panel and then to your lights and electronics. Installing something, such as replacing a broken GPS or adding some LED lighting, is typically just a matter of wiring it into the system. We're not going to discuss 120-volt shore power systems which offer higher risk to do-it-yourselfers. For work on 120-volt systems, you'd be wise to consult a marine electrician.

The key with wiring on a boat is realizing that it needs to be more durable than household wiring due to the potential for corrosion and the movement found on boats. Use tinned marine grade wires and connectors. Ancor brand makes a very good selection of wiring, connectors, and crimping tools. Equally important is what not to use. Don't use common household wire nuts or just twist the ends of wire together with some electrical tape. House wiring is solid core and easily fatigues with boat movement and vibration. Proper marine wires have fine strands.

If you're used to automotive wiring, there are a few important differences. Cars often use single wires for the power supply, and the ground wire is replaced by a connection to the body of the car. Boats use double wires, encased in a common jacket, one positive, and one negative. Red wires are positive, and black (or sometimes yellow on newer boats) are negative. European-built boats may use an alternate color coding, with blue as positive and brown for negative—but check with the manufacturer.

Basic Boat Wiring Tips

If you add electrical equipment, make sure the wire or cable is the correct size. (Installation directions will often include this information.) If not, there are boat wiring tables available online to give you guidance.

Turn off the power before starting work by removing the positive battery cable or switching off the battery switch.

If the item you are wiring is not already running to a circuit breaker or fuse, you'll want to add one to your panel using the size recommendations by the equipment manufacturer. The positive wire will be attached to the breaker or fuse, and the negative wire goes to the negative ground buss bar.

Keep a record of any new wires, cables, or electrical equipment you install. Having a wiring diagram can help you troubleshoot later.

The ends of the wire connecting to the breaker panel will normally use ring connectors, where the breaker screw goes through a ring of the connector. I'd recommend crimp connectors and a high-quality crimping tool. Unless you're an expert, it's easy to mess up a solder connection. Tug on the connector after it's crimped to make sure it's securely attached to the wire. The other end of the wire may use butt connectors, where a wire enters from each end. This is typical for equipment that comes with a short pigtail of two wires, like a bilge pump or a light. But other items may have screw terminals, so use ring connectors on them. In between the two ends, secure the wire every 18 inches or so to the boat structure using cable ties. Make sure you avoid sharp corners where the wire could chafe.

Installing a New Cabin Light

There are a variety of simple electrical projects that your boat might need; one common one is installing a new cabin light. The first step is to plan where the fixture is going to go and how you will get the wire from the breaker panel to the light. Choose the correct size of wire for the current draw of the light, and the length of wire required. Mount the light and run the new wire from the breaker or fuse panel to the light.

Here are some suggestions for books if you're going to do these types of jobs yourself:

Brotherton, Miner and Ed Sherman. *The 12-Volt Bible for Boats.* (Camden: McGraw-Hill, 2002).

Calder, Nigel. *Boatowner's Mechanical and Electrical Manual.* (Camden: McGraw-Hill, 1996).

Miller, Conrad and E. S. Maloney. *Your Boat's Electrical System.* (Hearst Books; Rev Sub edition, 1988).

Sherman, Ed. *Powerboater's Guide to Electrical Systems.* (Camden: McGraw-Hill, 2007).

Wing, Charlie. *Boatowner's Illustrated Handbook of Wiring.* (Camden: McGraw-Hill, 1993).

Replacing a Halyard

On a recent sailing trip, my husband mentioned that the genoa halyard was getting on in years. He also mentioned it felt a bit stiff, looked a bit chafed in places, and that it was probably nearly time to replace it with a new one. A short while later, the halyard broke.

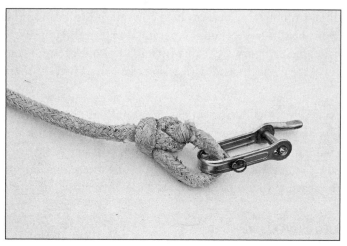

A worn halyard.

Halyards are much easier to replace before they break, and the process is pretty straightforward. The goal is to use the old halyard to pull the new one into place. But before you can do that, you need to get your new halyard completely ready to go and you need to find a secure way to attach the two halyards together. Do the following:

- Cut the snap shackle (where you attach the sail head) off your old halyard.

- Then either tie this snap shackle onto the new halyard or get a rigger to splice it on. (We prefer to tie, because chafe often happens near the pulley at the top of the mast, where the shackle ends up when the sail is up, and if the halyard is tied, you can easily cut off a few inches and move the knot along as required.)

- Sew the (nonshackle) end of the new halyard to the cut in the old one. Do this by cutting out some of the old halyard's core and then inserting the new halyard under the remaining cover (remember, halyards are often made of double braid, so there is a core and a cover—see Chapter 12 for more detail). Sew the halyards together with sailmaker's thread. Make this as tidy as possible so the join doesn't get hung up as you thread it through the mast.

Then give it a couple of tight wraps with electrical tape to cover any loose threads.

- Gently pull the old halyard up through the mast. This will gradually pull the new halyard into place. Be sure not to pull the shackle up off the deck.

But if you did what we did and waited until the halyard broke, you'll need to thread a messenger line through your mast to help you out. This means either lowering your mast, or, if your boat is large enough, making a trip to the top of the mast. From the top of the mast, feed a lightweight line through the halyard pulley and then drop it down the mast (weight the end with a short length of bicycle chain or a stack of washers).

When the weight hits the bottom of the mast, pull it out the opening in the side of the mast. The person at the top of the mast might need to pull it up and down a bit to make it swing into view. A flashlight and bent coat hanger are helpful to get it out. Then sew the new halyard to other end of the messenger line and pull it up the outside of the mast, through the pulley, and down the inside of the mast.

SAILOR'S WARNING

Always keep the working end of a halyard (the shackle end) clipped to either a sail, the deck, or some other secure point. Shackles that are left free to swing can injure people and they can also start to snake their way up the mast—making them very difficult to retrieve.

A note about going up the mast: going up the mast isn't for novices. You need to have the correct gear and be shown how to go up and down safely:

- Always use a bosun's chair or climbing harness.
- Tie the halyard to the bosun's chair with a bowline; don't use the shackle, because they can break or spring open. Check the security of your knot by bouncing with your full weight in the chair at deck level.
- Always use a safety line. This is a second halyard, so that if the first line fails you're still safe.
- Carry your tools in a secure bag, not in a pocket, as they could fall on the person below.
- Plan (in advance) communication with whoever is doing the hoisting.

- If you are standing below, stand clear while the person up the mast is working to avoid being hit if something is dropped.

- Use a winch to pull the person up the mast. On smaller boats you'll need to lead the halyard back to the cockpit where the largest winches can be found.

- If using a self-tailing winch, *do not* rely on that alone as a "cleat" as that has resulted in people falling from aloft. Instead, when the desired height is reached and with the halyard still on the winch, tie the tail to a sturdy cleat.

Replacing an Impeller

Beyond changing the engine fluids, one of the most common engine maintenance items is changing the cooling water pump impeller (the small rubber rotating part inside the pump that moves the water). But *when* to replace the impeller tends to come with a variety of opinions and recommendations. Some manufacturers say you should replace the impeller every year, often after winter lay-up. Most of us don't—which means we replace them when they fail.

Impeller pumps generally fail in one of two ways. The first mode of failure is less noticeable because of a gradual decrease in pump performance. The second type of failure is more catastrophic—and the impeller usually looses some or all of its blades. This can happen when an impeller pump runs dry. (The fluid being pumped provides the cooling and lubrication for the pump.) The cause of this failure is when someone forgets to open a cooling water seacock or the intake gets plugged with a plastic bag.

 SAILOR'S WARNING

When the impeller sheds its blades because of failure, missing blades need to be tracked down and removed from the system. Keep in mind that failing to find them can lead to further problems and blockages later on. So be sure all the blades are accounted for. They will usually be found in the entrance to the engine heat exchanger.

Outboard engine pumps are probably the most difficult to maintain. Changing the impeller requires separating the lower gear case from the engine, and you can't change this impeller on the water. Consult your engine manual for the specific steps required to get to the pump because it is much more involved than inboard engines.

In contrast, inboard boat engines impellers are easy to change. All you'll need are the spare impeller, a wrench to remove the pump from its bracket, and a screwdriver to remove the pump cover plate.

You'll need to close the intake seacock first. Then unscrew the cover plate from the pump to expose the impeller. On some engines you have to loosen the V-belt and unbolt the pump to gain access to the cover plate. Some impellers slide onto the central pump shaft, and some have a little set screw holding them in place, which will be need to be removed first.

The pump will often use a paper gasket (which you have to scrape off gently so as to not scratch the metal surface it's stuck to, and replace with the one that comes with the new impeller). Some pump covers use an O-ring which you can reuse. Gently bend the blades of the impeller to fit inside the pump body, replace the gasket or O-ring, and tighten up the cover plate. If you had to remove the pump from the engine, you'll need to tighten up the pump V-belt and tighten the mounting bolts. Finally, open the seacock and you're back in business.

The Least You Need to Know

- Developing a few basic repair and maintenance skills will help make the do-it-yourself aspect of boat ownership more enjoyable.
- When fixing fiberglass, premixed fillers may be worth the extra money because they are easier to use than epoxies you mix by hand.
- Finding a leak can be tricky, but not impossible, if you keep an eye out for telltale signs (like rust), and use hoses and washable markers to determine the origin/direction of water flow for hard-to-locate leaks.
- When replacing wiring, use tinned marine-grade wires rather than wiring made for residential or automobile use.
- Replacing a worn halyard proactively is much easier than waiting for it to break.
- Changing the impeller before it wears out can save time and effort and is better for your engine.

Finding the Right Boat

In This Chapter

- Selecting the right boat for right now
- Determining what can you afford
- Going with new or used
- Knowing when to walk away or say yes!

When we told people we wanted to buy a sailboat, the first thing they said (no doubt while imagining us sipping cocktails and sailing past a tropical island) was, "You must be rich." Then the clichés started coming: "Boats are holes in the water where you pour your money." "The second happiest day in your life is the day you buy your boat and the happiest will be the day you sell it."

Sure, rich people own boats—but most people with sailboats own them because they like sailing. Think about the cost this way: a trailerable day sailor that you launch from a boat ramp can cost less than an annual vacation to somewhere warm, while a cruising boat that sleeps five and is kept in a marina can be more affordable than a family cottage.

When it comes to budgeting for a boat, the cost depends on the size and type of boat, where you keep it, and how you'll use it. These costs can vary—making it possible to fit a boat into just about any budget. But the key to affording the right boat is to calculate the true cost of boat ownership, not just the cost of your monthly loan payment.

Choosing the Best Type of Boat for You

There is an endless variety of boats out there, and the first step in finding yours is deciding what kind of vessel suits your needs—right now. Most new buyers look at boats as a long-term investment, but statistics show that typical ownership lasts about 4 years. So, while you may dream about heading off and cruising the Caribbean someday, you'll probably get better use out of a boat that meets your needs during the summer weekends you have available this year.

When trying to decide on the right kind of boat, consider the following questions.

Will a small boat do?

- Are you planning to mess around on the water on sunny afternoons with your kids, or go for beachside picnics?

- Are you planning to use the boat in sheltered waterways or on lakes?

- Do you want to trailer the boat or park it at home?

A sailing dinghy is a great choice for families wanting to experience the pure fun of sailing.
(Evan Gatehouse)

DEFINITION

A **dinghy**, or tender, is a small boat for sailboats that might be anchored or moored away from shore. It can also be a small open sailing boat that's used for recreation.

Maybe you want a larger boat?

- Do you have a large family or love to throw BBQs?

- Do you plan to go cruising for long weekends, or cross exposed bodies of water?

- Do you plan to keep the boat in a marina and entertain dockside?

- Do you have friends who you can bribe to help paint the bottom?

A small cruising catamaran might be the perfect choice for a couple or family that wishes to cruise on weekends or extended trips.

(Evan Gatehouse)

How will you use your boat?

- Are you a fair-weather boater who will boat only on sunny summer days?

- Will you be cooking and sleeping aboard?

- Do you want to compete in local races with friends?

- Do your skills match the boat you are looking at, or will you need additional training?

Conventional wisdom says to start with a small boat, such as a dinghy, and then hone your skills and move up. This is a great plan if you have kids or if a dinghy is what you want. But dinghies capsize, and often a small daysailer gets more use. A boat in the 18- to 27-foot range is still simple to sail, roomy enough for guests or a family, safe enough for changing conditions, and is affordable.

Keep in mind that sailing skills can develop quickly once you start sailing frequently, so consider a boat you'll grow into. Check what boats are popular in your local waters—these will typically be boats that can manage the local conditions well.

Once you've narrowed down the type of boat you want, you can start to look for one that meets your budget.

What Kind of Boat Can You Afford?

You've decided on your dream boat, so now you need to figure out if you can actually afford it. Keep in mind the purchase price is just the beginning—boats cost money to store, outfit, run, and insure.

You'll need to ask yourself: What kind of budget do you have for getting started and how much can you spend annually? How much will it cost to moor, insure, and maintain the boat you are considering? How much upgrading is required to get the boat into good condition? What kind of cool extras will you want (BBQ, radar, heater, dinghy, stereo, or fishing gear)?

Here's a table to help you calculate the approximate annual cost of boat ownership for three typical entry-level boats that a new sailor might be interested in purchasing. The options vary, ranging from a used trailer boat that doesn't require financing to new a new dinghy or small cruising boat that might.

Calculate Your Annual Cost of Boat Ownership

Expenses	Hunter 15' dinghy owned in Florida	26' Macgregor used in Washington	22' Sport Catalina new in Maryland
Cost of Boat	$8,000 new ($5,000 used)	$6,500 used ($22,000 new)	$21,000 new ($6,000 used)
Monthly Payments × 12	$1,020	N/A	$2,664
Insurance Premiums	Covered by household	$130	$540
Registration and Licensing Fees	$36	$42	$26
Needed Upgrades	$350 (4 PFDs, VHF radio, oars)	$750 (new main sail)	N/A
Desired Equipment (BBQ, sun awning, etc.)	$1,500 (trailer)	$700 (dinghy)	$2,000 (dinghy, life-jackets, VHF radio, safety equipment)
Moorage Fees	$550 for yard storage and boat ramp	$2,700	$3,500
Maintenance/ Repairs	$150	$600	$700
Fuel and Oil	N/A	$100	$100
Winter Storage (if needed)	N/A	N/A	$1,045
Total	$3,606	$11,022 the first year $5,022 for future years	$10,575

Boat costs will vary widely based on your region, the type of boat you purchase, the equipment you purchase, and how you use it. The above table is simply a guideline.

NAUTICAL KNOWLEDGE

Surveyors estimate that getting a secondhand boat into shipshape condition can range from 10 percent of the purchase price for a basic day sailor in good condition, to as much as 100 percent of the purchase price for an older, more complex sailboat that needs new sails and most of her systems replaced.

Boat Loans and Insurance

If you're not buying your boat outright, you'll need to finance it. Comparing your loan options online is a good way to start. And remember, just like any loan, you can save money in the long run by paying a larger down payment and keeping the term as short as possible.

You can also research the cost of boat insurance online. The amount you'll pay for insurance varies by the boat's value, where you're using it, the level of coverage you require, and courses you've taken or experience you may have. Some small boats can be covered by a rider on your homeowner's policy—but check to see if this is the most affordable option.

When we were shopping for insurance for our boat, the first policy we looked at was incomprehensible, as was the second. Once we got a handle on the lingo, though, we discovered that subtle-sounding differences in language could mean some big differences in potential claim payouts.

The first big difference between policies is *agreed value* versus *actual cash value*. Agreed value policies are more expensive, but actual cash policies mean your boat or equipment could be paid out at a very low value.

DEFINITION

Agreed value is the value of your vessel as agreed on by you and your insurance broker (often set by an insurance survey). This is the amount you'll be paid if you experience a total loss.

Actual cash value is the replacement cost of your vessel or equipment, less the depreciation, as determined by the insurer at the time of your loss.

Beyond the value issue there is the question of damage caused by wear, tear, and gradual deterioration or corrosion versus damage caused by an accident. This might not sound like a big deal, but if a piece of worn or corroded equipment breaks, the result can be catastrophic (imagine a fitting that holds up the mast breaking—the mast comes down, sails may be torn, the deck may sustain damage). But with consequential wear and tear coverage, everything but the fitting that broke would be covered.

Other details to be aware of are exclusions, navigation limits, and deductible options. Once you understand all your options, check if your broker has any "value added" items or discounts available. Some policies have breakdown towing while others offer discounts for taking boating courses or adding safety equipment.

Storage

Sometimes storing a boat can cost more than a monthly loan payment. Full-service marinas and yacht clubs (some include onsite shops, restaurants, clubhouses, swimming pools, and other amenities) tend to be the most expensive option. But if you're the sort of sailor that enjoys the convenience, services, and oftentimes the built-in social life that comes with life in a yacht club, then the expense will be worth it.

Marinas are convenient moorage and come with a variety of amenities and in a range of costs.
(Evan Gatehouse)

A less-expensive option for storing your boat is in a *mooring* field or at anchor. This is not always the most secure way to leave a boat if you plan to leave it for long periods. You also need to be aware of local regulations which may limit the amount of time you can be at anchor.

DEFINITION

A **mooring** is an on-the-water storage area with permanent mooring buoys that you attach your boat to.

If you have a small boat, you might choose to keep it on a trailer in your backyard, which you then launch from a nearby boat ramp. Keep in mind you'll need a vehicle rated for towing a boat and should double-check your local bylaws and covenants before planning to store a boat at home. The benefit is that, with the right boat and trailer setup, you can explore far-flung areas simply by driving to them *and* then launching your boat.

Anchorages and mooring fields are a popular low-cost alternative.
(Evan Gatehouse)

Another small boat or winter alternative is yard storage. A typical storage facility will keep your boat on cradles and then launch it when you need it.

Maintenance and Running Costs

It can be challenging for a first-time boat owner to know exactly how much a boat will cost to maintain. Basic day sailors of simple construction don't cost a lot of money in upkeep. Most only require the occasional replacement of ropes and sails, and are easy to repair. Larger boats with wood trim that requires varnish, hulls that need waxing, and complex mechanical systems that wear out require more money and more time to maintain.

One way to lower maintenance costs is to do the work yourself. But whether you do some work on your own, or have your boat serviced, the basic boat maintenance costs you'll need to budget for are cleaning supplies, engine, hull and sail servicing, and emergency repairs.

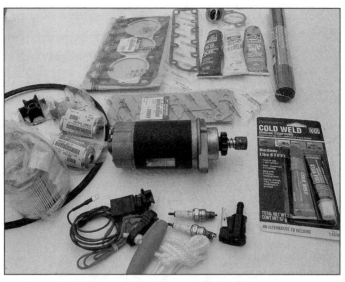

You'll save money in the long run if you learn to do your own maintenance—but initially you'll need to buy tools and spare parts.
(Evan Gatehouse)

Outfitting

One area that's easy to miss in your budget is planning for outfitting. New boats often come with a variety of equipment packages, but they don't come with personal items or the kind of gear that make boat ownership more fun—including different sails for different conditions, dinghies for larger boats, and some electronics.

One good way to save on outfitting costs is to spread out your shopping and look for bargains in the off-season or during boat shows. Keep in mind that buying bargain brands for essentials including anchors, dinghies, and safety equipment won't be a good value if the items don't stand up to long-term marine use.

Personal items such as foul weather gear (nautical speak for raincoat and pants) will make boating more enjoyable for the whole family.
(Evan Gatehouse)

New Versus Pre-Owned

Just like buying a car, there are benefits to both new and pre-owned boats. New boats give you access to innovative technology and the latest designs, as well as state-of-the-art electronics and modern mechanical systems. New boats also come with hull and engine warranties—a detail that doesn't guarantee headache-free ownership, but that does mean you at least get to share your headaches.

On the flip-side, used boats are cheaper. And a boat that starts out with a lower sticker price also costs less for insurance and will have lower monthly payments. Another advantage of a pre-owned boat is you'll have a wider range of brands, models, and layouts to choose between. But you're pretty much on your own with the headaches.

SAILOR'S WARNING

Extra equipment, including ground tackle, dinghy, depth sounder, or radar, are often not reflected in the purchase price of a used boat but are expensive to add. Check out comparable boats and add up the cost of what isn't included.

Where to Find the Boat of Your Dreams

Know the saying, before you find your prince you need to kiss a lot of frogs? Well, the same could be said for boats. Chances are, before you find *your* boat you're going to need to kick a lot of nautical tires. The initial stages of shopping should be about learning, so get out and see as many boats as you can, read as many reviews as you can, and get as much information as you can process.

Boat Shows

Perhaps the best place of all to start is at a boat show. Not only do boat shows have boats (which you can crawl around and explore every nook and cranny of), but they also have boating gear, boating information, and many offer workshops and seminars covering all manner of boating education. Boat shows come in a variety of sizes and focuses, so it may be worth checking what shows are occurring in both your immediate region and beyond.

Boat Reviews

Not every boat will have been reviewed, but if you are looking at a common production boat, chances are it has, several times. If you've narrowed down your interest to a handful of boats, start hunting down their reviews—you can find them online or in the archives of major sailing magazines. Most are written by journalists who have made a career out of looking at boats, so a good review should pick up details that you may not have thought about and point out a boat's pros and cons.

Check out your regional sailing magazines for information as well. Regional magazines typically do fewer reviews—but the boats they focus on are the ones that are suited to local conditions.

Boat Brokers

Consider enlisting the help of a boat broker. Unlike used-car salesmen, boat brokers are more interested in finding you the right boat than simply selling something in their inventory. But keep in mind, brokers tend to specialize. Some brokers work primarily with people selling offshore yachts, while others focus on the luxury market, powerboats, or multihulls.

There are two ways to use a broker. You can contact the listing broker (the broker representing the seller) when you see a boat that interests you, or you can select a broker of your own who will help you find a boat. Either way, the broker's role is the same—they should let you know about the condition and history of the boat before you go see it. And they'll help you determine a realistic offer for a used boat.

What to Look For in Your Future Boat

Never underestimate the power of love. Many people will tell you not to buy something just because you fell in love with it, but honestly, boats are a bit mystical and unless there is that element of love involved, I'd keep looking. Once you find a boat that makes your heart flutter, your bank account say "sure," and your family and friends cheer, it's time to look more closely.

Cosmetic flaws such as faded paint, old brown plaid upholstery, and an ill-equipped head or galley are easy and fairly affordable fixes. Other issues need more attention.

Proceed with caution if you encounter the following:

- Mismatched paint. This could indicate that the boat has been in an accident and had repairs made.

- Warped or bent keel or rudder. The boat may have been in a collision.

- Apparent water line stains inside the boat or on the engine. This could indicate that the boat took on water.

- Soft spots on the deck. These can indicate the separation of layers of fiberglass cloth and resin from each other or from the boat's core layers, which is known as delamination. It's usually caused by physical stress to the boat's fiberglass surface.

- Water stains around hatches and windows. This can indicate leaks.

- Musty/moldy smell inside. This could indicate prior water damage or simple neglect.

- Recurring problems in the maintenance records (or no records). This can indicate a problem area or inadequate maintenance.

SAILOR'S WARNING

Before buying a boat, check that the Hull Identification Number (HIN) matches the number on the registration documents. Thieves will often modify a HIN to hide that they are trying to sell you a stolen boat.

Getting a Second Opinion: Surveys and Sea Trials

If you're still in love and everything looks good, for most boats the next step is to hire a surveyor. The exception to this would be mass-produced boats under about 20 feet and about $3,000—but even those may require an insurance survey. An insurance survey is similar to an inspection survey but often less intensive. Typically the boat owner selects an approved surveyor who then inspects the condition of the boat and sets a value for the boat. This value is typically open for discussion.

In most cases an inspection survey will include hauling out, so make sure you have an entire day available to devote to the exercise. The surveyor will examine the boat and all her systems. (Be sure to point out anything that gave you concern.) Most will not inspect the engine(s) (so hire a mechanic for that), and often a sail maker can give a better assessment of the sails and a rigger can give you a better idea about the condition of the mast, stays, and shrouds.

Most surveyors will find multiple things wrong with a boat. This doesn't mean you chose badly—it's simply an opportunity to gather information and decide if the boat's underlying flaws are large enough, or costly enough, to repair that you want to walk away from the deal. The more typical scenario is to approach the owner with the list of problems and the anticipated cost for repairs and then renegotiate the price based on the new information.

Sea trials can be done before or after the survey and are usually done with your boat broker. What you are looking for depends on what you enjoy. With a sailboat you'll want to know how she sails in both light air and gusty/choppy conditions.

NAUTICAL KNOWLEDGE

It's well known that renaming a boat can bring bad luck. But with a traditional renaming ceremony, where you ask the four brother winds for protection and pour a generous serving of champagne overboard as an offering, you can rename your boat without fear of angering the gods. and if you've bought a new boat, you can use the same ceremony to bring good luck and fair weather to your sailing days. Sure it's superstitious, but as every sailor knows, it's better to be safe than sorry.

The Least You Need to Know

- Finding the right boat is easier when you know exactly how you'll want to use it right now.
- Working out what you can afford means calculating the boat loan plus the annual costs of ownership.
- Both new boats and used boats have pros and cons worth considering.
- Working with a boat broker, insurance broker, and surveyor can help demystify the boat-buying process and ensure you get what you want.

Glossary

abeam   A direction away from the side of the boat.

actual cash value   A type of insurance policy that provides a depreciated replacement cost for a total loss, much like a car insurance policy.

advisory   A significant weather event is possible in your area.

affirmative   Radio call: means yes.

aft   The back of the boat.

agreed value   A type of insurance policy that provides a previously agreed amount if the boat is a total loss.

AIS   Automatic Identification System, a radio system that allows ships to broadcast information about their course and speed. Recreational sailors can receive these messages on AIS receivers to help avoid collisions.

altocumulus clouds   Small clumpy clouds resembling fish scales in the sky that often precede cold fronts.

anchor rode   The length of line or chain that is used to attach an anchor to a boat.

antifouling   Special paint applied to the underwater part of boats stored in the water that prevents marine growth on the hull.

apparent wind   Combination of two winds: the true wind and the one created by your boat's motion.

autopilot   A device which steers your boat.

backing the jib   Pulling the jib sheet to the opposite side of the boat so the jib fills with wind on its reverse side.

backstay   The rearmost wire that holds up the mast and is attached to the stern.

bailer   Some sort of bucket or scoop for removing water from a boat.

battens Thin strips of fiberglass inserted in the mainsail that support the sail's roach.

beam The widest part of a boat.

beam reach A point of sail where the wind comes over the beam and the sails are halfway out.

bearing off Turning the boat away from the wind.

bight A bend in a rope.

bimini An awning that covers some or all of a cockpit and protects from the sun or rain.

binnacle A post or pedestal in front of the steering wheel that often houses navigational instruments.

block and tackle An arrangement of blocks (pulleys) and lines used to pull or hoist.

boat hook A hook on the end of a long pole.

bolt rope A rope sewn into an edge of a sail.

boom Horizontal tube that extends back from near the base of the mast. Bottom of mainsail is attached to it.

boom vang A control line or tackle that pulls the boom down.

boot stripe The stripe where bottom paint and the topside paint meet.

bow roller A storage place for the anchor on the bow.

bowline A favorite sailing knot that forms a fixed loop.

bowman The person who works on the front of the boat, taking down foresails and getting spinnakers ready to deploy and retrieve.

broad reach A point of sail where the wind comes over the stern quarter, sails are well out, and the boat is angled at about 135 degrees from the wind.

bulkhead A vertical wall on a boat.

cat's paws Dark ruffled patches on the water that indicate a gust of wind.

centerboard A fin under the hull that provides lift. It can pivot upward into the hull.

chafe Ropes or sails being damaged by rubbing against something.

chainplate   A metal fitting bolted to the hull or deck that mast rigging wires are attached to.

chandlery   Store where nautical products and supplies are sold.

chocks   Fittings for a running line.

cirrocumulus clouds   Thin white wisps with a hint of fluffy white clouds are a sign of fine sailing weather to come.

cirrostratus clouds   Thin veil-like layers of clouds; may be a sign that rain is on its way.

cirrus clouds   High wispy clouds that signal a weather change.

cleat   A fitting used to hold a rope securely.

clew   Back bottom corner of the sail.

close hauled   A point of sail where you are sailing as close to the wind as possible while still keeping the sails filled with wind. Sails will be pulled in tight.

close reach   A point of sail where the wind comes from about 50 degrees off the bow and sails are pulled in quite tight.

coil   To stow a length of line into circular loops.

Colregs   The Collision Regulations which outline rules of the road.

companionway   Opening into a sailboat's cabin.

compass   A basic navigational instrument that points to magnetic north.

compass rose   Circular angle markings on a chart indicating true north and magnetic north.

cumulonimbus clouds   Towering dark cumulus clouds that are usually associated with squalls and lightning.

cumulus clouds   Fluffy white clouds that commonly indicate fine sailing weather.

cunningham   A control line that pulls down on the mainsail luff.

current table   Book of current predictions for an area.

daggerboard   A fin under the hull that provides lift. It can be lifted vertically into the hull.

datum   Level of water that depths are measured from.

daybeacons   Navigational markers on posts.

dead reckoning   To establish one's position from a starting point knowing speed and direction travelled.

depth sounder   An electronic instrument that measures water depth.

Digital Selective Calling (DSC)   A feature of modern radios that allows for automated distress calls as well as private calls to another boat.

dinghy   A small boat used to go from your larger boat to shore; sometimes called a tender. Also a small open sailboat used for racing and recreation.

dividers   Handheld geometry instrument used to measure distances on charts.

dodger   An enclosure for the front of the cockpit and companion that protects from wind, rain, or spray; often made of canvas and with a clear vinyl window to see through.

double braid   A type of rope construction with an inner core and outer braided cover.

down below   Inside a sailboat's cabin.

downwind run   A point of sail where the wind is coming from directly astern and sails are all the way out, or you are wing on wing.

draft   The depth of the deepest part of the boat. Also, the fullness of a sail.

drag anchor   When an anchor fails to hold the boat in position and slides along the bottom without catching.

east cardinal buoy   Buoy that marks safest water to the east.

ebb tide   Water going down toward low tide.

EPIRB   Emergency Position Indicating Radio Beacon. A radio distress beacon.

fairleads   A fitting with a smooth inner surface to change the direction of a rope.

fairway buoy   Buoy that marks the middle of a channel.

fall off   Turning the boat away from the wind.

fenders   Soft bumpers that protect your boat at a dock.

fix   To find a position using a compass bearing on two or more objects on shore, or using a sextant, or using electronic navigational equipment.

float plan   A plan of your voyage left with family or friends.

flood tide Water rising toward a high tide.

fogging oil Special oil sprayed into an engine to preserve it during months of nonuse.

foghorn function A VHF radio function that can sound automatic foghorn signals through an external horn.

forestay The forwardmost wire that holds up the mast and is attached to the bow.

fouled ground A sea bottom unsuitable for anchoring due to some hazard.

furling system A sail storage system in which the sail is wrapped around the forestay, mast, or boom and unwound as needed.

Gale Warning Warns of winds of 34 to 47 knots.

gelcoat Pigmented resin that forms the glossy outside surface of a boat.

genoa Larger forward sail, usually overlaps back past the mast.

give-way vessel The vessel designated to alter its course and speed when a collision is possible.

Global Maritime Distress Safety System (GMDS) An international system of communication that aids in maritime rescues.

GPS Global Positioning System. A system of satellites and user-operated receivers to provide your location and speed on the water.

grind Using a winch to tighten a line.

halyard The line used to hoist sails.

hanks Metal clips that attach the front edge of a jib to the forestay.

haul out Lifting a boat out of the water using a travel lift or other means.

head A marine toilet. Also the top corner of a sail.

head up, heading up Turning the boat closer to the wind.

head-to-wind Pointing directly into the wind.

heeling When the boat tips over in response to the pressure of wind on its sails.

helmsman The person who drives the boat and calls out commands.

hitch A knot that encircles a post or other (usually) round object.

hull Main structure of the boat.

Hurricane Warning Hurricane conditions (sustained winds of 63 knots or higher) are coming.

in irons Pointing directly into the wind.

isolated danger buoy Buoy that marks an isolated hazard.

jack stands Props to support a boat stored on land.

jibing Turning the stern of the boat through the wind so that the wind changes from one side of the boat to the other.

kedging off To use an anchor to pull a vessel into deeper water.

keel Heavy fin or foil under a boat that provides stability and lift.

knot A unit of speed: 1 nautical mile per hour.

knot meter An electronic instrument that measures boat speed through the water.

large-scale chart A chart that shows a large amount of detail but covers a small area.

latitude The north or south distance from the earth's equator to a particular location.

leeward The direction opposite to the way the wind is currently blowing.

lift Air pressure on sails that produces a driving force to move the boat forward.

light sequence Pattern of flashes a navigational light shows.

lines Ropes used to control sails.

listing broker The boat broker offering a boat for sale.

longitude The east or west distance from the Prime Meridian in Greenwich, England, to a particular location.

loop A circle of rope, used while tying knots.

lubber line A fixed line on a compass display that points to the front of the boat.

luff The forward end of the sail, and a term used to describe a sail that is flapping.

lull Area of light wind.

main trimmer The person who adjusts the sheets that control the mainsail.

marine forecasts Weather forecasts that emphasize wind and wave conditions.

mast The long slender vertical tube that sails are attached to.

Mayday   An emergency radio call that is placed when there is imminent danger to life or to the continued viability of the vessel.

mooring field   On-the-water storage area with many boats secured to permanent mooring buoys.

neap tides   Smallest tides that happen during the first and last quarters of the moon.

negative   Radio call: means no.

north cardinal buoy   Buoy that marks safest water to the north.

no-sail zone   An area too close to the wind or pointing almost directly into the wind where a boat cannot sail.

on the hard   A boat that is stored on land.

out   Radio call: means my radio call is finished.

outhaul   The control line that attaches to the mainsail clew.

over   Radio call: means my transmission is over and it's the other party's turn to speak.

over canvassed   When the boat has too much sail up.

painter   A line used on the bow of a dinghy to secure it to a dock or a boat.

Pan Pan   An urgent radio call that is one step below a Mayday emergency call with danger to property or safety.

parallel ruler   Used to transfer a course on a chart to or from the compass rose on the chart.

Personal flotation device (PFD)   A flotation device or lifejacket.

Personal Location Beacon (PLB)   A distress beacon similar to an EPIRB, but smaller and with shorter battery life.

pitman   The person who works with the bowman who stows sails below deck and hoists sails.

plot   Marking your position on a chart.

points of sail   A term describing the various angles at which the wind hits the sails and what the corresponding sail shapes should be.

port   Left-hand side of the boat, as you are facing forward.

port junction (bifurcation) buoy   Buoy that marks preferred channel. Keep the port bouy on your port side (when facing upstream).

port trimmer   The person who controls the foresail and the spinnaker on the port side of the boat.

port-hand buoy   Buoy that marks the left-hand side of a channel (when facing upstream).

prop walk   The sideways motion of the stern of the boat due to propeller thrust.

protractor   Handheld geometry instrument used to plot compass courses and bearings on charts.

radar   A navigational aid that uses radio waves to provide a picture of your surroundings.

rail meat   The unskilled crew members on a race boat whose primary function is to act as moveable ballast.

reaching   The points of sail including close, beam, and broad reaching.

reef   Reduce the size of sails.

relative bearing   The compass angle between your boat and another vessel or feature on shore.

roach   The back part of the mainsail or headsail that extends past a straight line between clew and head.

roger   Radio call: means understood.

roller furling   *See* furling system.

rope clutch   A fitting used to secure a line.

rudder   Moveable foil at the back of the boat that steers the boat.

running rigging   The adjustable ropes and lines that control the sails.

scale   Ratio between distance on a chart and the actual distance it represents.

scope   The amount of anchor rode or chain used or the ratio of the length of rope to water depth.

sea cocks   An underwater valve that lets in water (or allows water to drain out).

sea state   The condition of sea; how large the waves are.

secondary station   A VHF radio having an additional control microphone separate from the main radio.

Securite   A radio call that is placed to provide safety information to other boaters.

set   Dropping and positioning your anchor so that it digs in and holds.

shackle   A metal connecting link, usually with a screwed pin.

shakedown voyage   First trip after major repairs, modifications, or purchase of a new boat.

sheave   A pulley.

shrouds   Wires that hold up the mast that come to the sides of the boat.

skipper   The person who drives the boat and calls out commands.

slab reefing system   A method of reducing the mainsail size by lowering part of the sail and gathering up the bottom.

slack water   Times when the water movement or current is minimal.

slides   Plastic or metal fittings on the front edge of the mainsail that slide up the mast groove or track.

sloop   A sailboat with one mast and two sails, a mainsail and a foresail.

slugs   Plastic or metal fittings on the front edge of the mainsail that slide up the mast groove or track.

small craft   Smaller sailboats most likely to be affected by rough weather.

small craft Advisory   Winds of 22 to 33 knots that are hazardous to smaller sailboats.

small-scale chart   A chart that shows a small amount of detail but covers a large area.

sound signals   The use of a horn or whistle to indicate a ship's intentions.

south cardinal buoy   Buoy that marks safest water to the south.

Special Marine Warning (SMW)   Nonscheduled forecasts of sudden events that are short-lived but potentially dangerous.

Specific Area Message Encoding (S.A.M.E.)   A programmable VHF radio feature that alerts you to weather and other emergencies for the area you choose.

splice   To permanently join two parts of a rope by interlocking the fibers.

spoil area   An area of underwater debris noted on a chart.

SPOT   A satellite messaging device that can send simple messages and relay your position.

spreaders   Horizontal struts extending outward from the mast.

spring line   A line going from boat to dock used to stop the boat from moving forward or backward too much.

spring tides   Highest or lowest tides in a month.

stanchion   Vertical metal posts that support the lifelines around the perimeter of the boat.

standing end   Any rope that is leading away from the ends of a rope.

standing rigging   The collection of wires that hold up the mast.

stand-on vessel   The vessel designated to maintain its course and speed when a collision is possible.

starboard   Right-hand side of the boat, as you are facing forward.

starboard junction (bifurcation) buoy   Buoy that marks preferred channel. Keep the starboard bouy on your starboard side (when facing upstream).

starboard trimmer   The person who controls the foresail and the spinnaker on the starboard side of the boat.

Starboard-hand buoy   Buoy that marks the right-hand side of a channel (when facing upstream).

stays   Wires that extend forward and backward and hold up the mast that extend forward or backward.

stopper knot   A knot tied in the end of a line to keep the line from sliding through a fitting.

Storm Warning   Forecasted winds of 48 to 63 knots.

stuffing box   A shaft seal that prevents leaks between sliding or turning parts; often found on rudder and propeller shafts.

swing   A boat pivoting around the point where the anchor is secured to the bottom.

tack   Turning the boat through the wind; or bottom forward corner of a sail; or the side of the boat the wind is coming from.

tactician   The person who uses the wind, currents, and conditions to find the most favorable course while racing.

telltales   Short pieces of yarn that are tied to the shrouds or attached to sails to show wind direction and air flow on sails.

three-strand   A type of rope construction with three main bundles twisted around each other.

through hull   A plumbing or other fitting that penetrates the hull. Some let sea water in (engine cooling water fitting) or fresh water out (sink drain).

tidal range   The distance between the highest water level during a high tide and the lowest water level during low tide.

tide table   Book of tidal height predictions for an area.

transducer   The portion of the depth sounder or wind instrument that picks up information and relays it back to the display unit.

travel lift   A special lifting device to lift boats from the water using slings under the hull.

traveler   A track with a moveable car that holds one end of the mainsheet.

trim   Adjust the sails.

Tropical Storm Warning   An announcement that tropical storm conditions (winds of 48–63 knots) are coming.

watch   A weather event is not only likely, it will have a serious impact; a watch mounted timepiece; or a period of time a crew member is alert and on duty.

waypoint   A latitude and longitude point used for navigation.

Weather Alert   A VHF radio function that automatically notifies you of a special weather alert.

weigh anchor   Lifting the anchor from the sea floor.

west cardinal buoy   Buoy that marks safest water to the west.

windlass   A special winch (manual or electric) that raises the anchor and rode.

windward   The direction from where the wind is currently blowing.

wing on wing   When running downwind with the mainsail out on one side and the foresail sheeted out on the other.

working end   The end of a rope.

yellow buoy   Buoy that indicates caution.

zinc anode   A sacrificial metal used for corrosion control for metals immersed in water.

Resources

Resources for sailors run the gamut—there are great organizations, courses, websites, and books all available and all designed to help you feel more comfortable on the water. This listing is by no means exhaustive, but it may help you get started.

Sailing Schools

Most sailing schools in the U.S. and Canada are affiliated with one of these three governing bodies:

American Sailing Association
asa.com/find_a_sailing_school.html

US Sailing
sailingcertification.com

Canadian Yachting Association
sailing.ca

Safe Boating Classes

Safe boating classes are offered through a wide variety of programs:

Boat U.S. Foundation
boatus.com/foundation

National Association of State Boating Law Administrators
nasbla.org

National Safe Boating Council
safeboatingcouncil.org

United States Power Squadrons
usps.org

U.S. Coast Guard Auxiliary
cgaux.org

In Canada, check with Transport Canada for a list of accredited boating safety course providers.

Voluntary Safety Checks

Getting a voluntary safety check is a great way to ensure you have all the necessary safety equipment aboard.

U.S. Coast Guard Auxiliary
cgaux.org/vsc

Canadian Coast Guard Auxiliary
ccga-gcac.ca

Weather and Tide Resources

There are a variety of resources for tide and weather information:

Current tables in text form
tidesandcurrents.noaa.gov

National Oceanic and Atmospheric Administration (NOAA)
nws.noaa.gov/om/marine/home.htm

Passage Weather
passageweather.com

Tidal information
tidesandcurrents.noaa.gov

Weather Underground
wunderground.com

Tow Companies

Many boaters find that a membership with a tow company is a good investment:

Sea Tow
seatow.com

Tow Boat US
towboatus.com

Navigation Resources

Free navigation resources can be found in a variety of places:

Chart No. 1 in United States
nauticalcharts.noaa.gov/mcd/chartno1.htm

Collision Regulations
navcen.uscg.gov/?pageName=navRulesContent

United States Coast Pilots
nauticalcharts.noaa.gov/nsd/cpdownload.htm

U.S. Coast Guard's Light List
navcen.uscg.gov/?pageName=lightLists

Canadian Coastal Pilots
charts.gc.ca/publications/sd-in/sd-in-eng.asp

Chart No. 1 in Canada
charts.gc.ca/publications/chart1-carte1/index-eng.asp

First Aid Information

Every boat should have a first aid kit and first aid manual aboard. Make sure you pull it out and restock it at the beginning of each season and remember to check for old and expired items.

At a minimum include:

>30 bandages—assorted sizes
>
>6 Butterfly closure strips
>
>1 elastic bandage
>
>4 exam gloves
>
>10 gauze pads—assorted sizes
>
>2 gauze rolls
>
>1 instant cold pack
>
>1 roll medical tape
>
>6 wound wipes
>
>Afterbite sting stick

Antibiotic ointment

Diphenhydramine (Benadryl) for allergies

Ibuprofen

Motion sickness tablets

Scissors

Sunscreen

Tweezers

Recognizing Heat Illness

Heat exhaustion and heat stroke are two illnesses that are caused by getting too much sun while drinking too little water.

A person suffering from heat exhaustion may be pale, dizzy, nauseated, and sweaty, but still cool to the touch. In more severe cases, they may vomit. Resting in a cool, shaded place and drinking water can usually relieve heat exhaustion, but, if left untreated, it can lead to heat stroke.

Heat stroke (also called sun stroke) is a severe illness in which the body's temperature-control mechanism fails. Because heat stroke impairs the body's ability to sweat, a person with heat stroke will have flushed, warm, dry skin and an elevated body temperature. Heat stroke can cause disorientation, aggressiveness, and even unconsciousness.

Someone with heat stroke needs immediate medical care. While arranging for help, cool the person off by fanning or misting them with cool water and offering him or her sips of cool water.

Avoiding Hypothermia

Hypothermia sets in when the body's core temperature drops below 35°C. It can be caused by exposure to air or water. (And remember, even when the weather is warm, the water can be very cold.) Loss of body heat results in loss of dexterity, loss of consciousness, and can lead to loss of life. Because your body can cool down 25 times faster in water than in air, all boaters should have cold water survival skills:

- Wear a PFD, and huddle by tucking your chin into your chest, crossing your arms, and pulling your knees up to your chest.

- Conserve heat by limiting movement. Swimming causes you to lose heat faster than staying still, so don't try to swim unless you can reach a nearby boat or floating object, or if there is little chance you'll be found quickly.

- Get as much of your body out of the water as possible (on top of an overturned boat or anything that floats).

Becoming a Greener Boater

There are a number of ways you can reduce your environmental impact and help protect the places you love:

- Fill your fuel tanks slowly and carefully and use rags and absorbent pads to catch drips. Fuel expands as it warms, so don't fill the tank to the top and always fill portable tanks on shore.

- Limit deck and hull washing and use green cleaners.

- Never discharge sewage at the dock, in an anchorage, or in a sensitive area.

- Keep your bilge clean by using an oil-absorbent pad and recycling any oil it collects. Don't pump oily water overboard.

- Recycle while under way and don't throw garbage overboard.

Finding a Boating Store (Chandleries)

Depending on the size of your town or city, you may have a local marine store. If not, there are a number of mail-order suppliers. Here is a small selection of the better-known ones.

Defender
defender.com

Hamilton Marine
hamiltonmarine.com

Jamestown Distributors
jamestowndistributors.com

West Marine
westmarine.com

Finding a Boat Show

From small local shows that may focus on wooden boats, trailer boats, or other specialty sailboats to international shows where the big manufacturers debut their latest models, boat shows are a great way to get ideas and find deals on new gear:

NAUTYCAL Find a Boat Show
findaboatshow.net

United States Yacht Shows
usboat.com

Sailing Apps and Programs

Smartphones and tablets are turning out to be some of the newest resources for sailors, with apps that do everything from chart plotting to reminding you how to tie a specific knot. Keep in mind that your device is not waterproof, though—so be sure to get a good-quality, waterproof case for yours, if you do plan to use it aboard.

Apple-Based Apps

There are over 400 Apple-based apps for sailing, cruising, and racing. Here are some of the best of them. You'll need the GPS version of the iPad to work with some of these apps, such as the apps for chartplotting.

Chartplotting Apps

iNavX is the original and still one of the best navigation apps for the iPad. At $50, it is also one of the most expensive. NOAA raster charts are a free download. It is well-designed and concentrates on the essentials.

Navionics Marine & Lakes uses Navionics vector format for charting. This allows you to display tide, weather info, overlay satellite, and Bing images on the charts. There is a large database of marine "points of interest" (mostly nav-aid waypoints but also marina and anchorage info and photos). Cost: $35.

Another basic app that uses NOAA raster charts is iSailGPS. Not as full-featured as the higher-priced competition, it's still a good choice if you're on a budget. Cost: $7.99.

Weather Apps

If you have a favorite weather website (Weather Underground, The Weather Channel, AccuWeather, NOAA Weather Radio, etc.), there's probably an app version for it, and most are free.

PocketGrib is a compact weather data format. GRIB software converts data files into graphical maps often overlaid on charts. Several of the chartplotter apps overlay GRIB data on a chart. PocketGrib allows users to download, view, and analyze current and forecast global weather data such as wind, precipitation, pressure, temp, wave data, etc. Useful if you want to get into the details of weather. Cost: $0.99.

Tide and Current Apps

Many tide apps require an internet connection (either Wi-Fi or 3G) for current information. Several chartplotter apps such as iNavX and Navionics include tide information , so if you have the navigation apps, you won't need these other apps, but there are some good stand-alone tide and current apps.

AyeTides XL is one of the best of the tide apps, but the most expensive. It has graphic and textual display of tides and currents from NOAA. If you buy iNavX and this app, it will appear if you run iNavX. The tide database is within the app, so no web connection is needed. Cost: $9.99.

NOAA Buoy & Tide Data gives data from NOAA's National Data Buoy Center, including tide predictions near the buoy's location and wave heights, if the buoy has that equipment. It can be hard to locate a particular buoy by name. Cost: $1.99.

AIS (Automatic Identification System) Apps

MarineTraffic offers coverage of 2,000 ports worldwide, including good AIS coverage in the United States. You click on your area in a map and the local map shows speed, course, and names of vessels equipped with AIS transceivers. This app is a handy tool, but remember, it's not a full-function AIS device. So some ships might not show up if you are outside the range of the reporting ports. Cost: $3.99.

Miscellaneous Apps

Knot Guide HD is an excellent how-to-tie knots app. It has lots of colour pictures to guide you through the ropes. Cost: $2.99.

Marine Rules & Signals is a collection of Rules of the Road and Signals. It's fairly plain but well put together. Cost: $5.99.

Marine Chart Symbols, by the same publisher as Marine Rules & Signals, gives all the standard marine chart symbols, but it's easier to use than the free PDF downloads of Chart No. 1. Cost: $4.99.

Android Smartphone and Tablet Apps

If you have a non-Apple device, you haven't been left out of the digital sailing revolution. You'll need a smartphone or tablet with a GPS to access chartplotting functions. Here are a few suggestions for you:

Chartplotting Apps

Memory-Map is a low-cost Android chartplotter app, assuming your Android smartphone or tablet has an internal or external GPS receiver, and offers many navigational functions. It doesn't offer all the bells and whistles, but it does a good job of basic charting and waypoint setting. Cost: $19.98.

Navionics Marine & Lakes is another basic chartplotting app. It has a number of useful features, such as a tool for measuring distances between points, and when it's online it can get wind and tide information. The basic help screens are available even when offline. Cost: $9.99.

Weather Apps

Marine Weather Pro provides users access to marine weather forecasts and live station data using NOAA data in an easier-to-read format. It includes all U.S. coastal regions inshore and offshore, the Great Lakes, Alaska, and Hawaii, but not Canada. Cost: $2.99.

PredictWind offers detailed local wind forecasts on an hour–by-hour basis. Cost: Free.

Tide and Current Apps

Tide Prediction enables easy offline viewing of graphical tidal charts. The app gives tides for over 3,000 tide and current stations worldwide, but is limited to the United States, Canada, Mexico, United Kingdom, Germany, Netherlands, South Africa, Japan, Australia, and New Zealand. Cost: Free.

AIS Apps

MarineTraffic (see earlier) is also available on Android devices. Cost: $3.99.

Miscellaneous Apps

Animated Knots by Grog shows how knots are tied in simple, step-by-step photo animations. There is also an info button to get detailed descriptions about each knot's correct use, advantages and disadvantages, and other information. Cost: $4.99.

Rules of the Road has excellent graphics, a clean design, and accurate info. Great for learning who to avoid and what to do in collision situations. Cost: $2.99.

Index

C

M

N

R

T

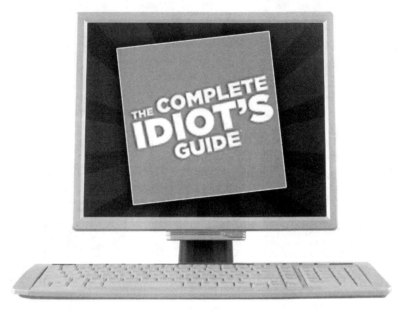

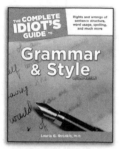

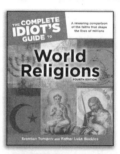

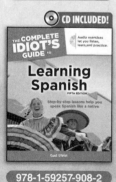

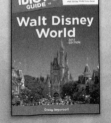